Freedom Management

Modern management theory has been established on the ashes of Taylorism, emphasizing control over accountability, conformity over uniqueness, and constraint over freedom. Leadership and management theories and the practical approaches of this age of society can be understood as an ongoing struggle to overcome the boundaries of such a concept of organizations and society. Also later movements, like empowerment or the competence-based waves of change have left what we do in organizations largely unscathed.

Organizations today are often bereft of a strong leadership function and the result is a decline in overall engagement. Luca Solari contends that this is because the change ahead requires a complete reshuffling of our conceptions of what it means to run an organization, and this will not come without pain for those in charge of managing, who are unable to shift their roles. It comes as no surprise that the complex pattern of pre-existing interests acts like a powerful shield against this change within government, society, and business organizations alike. This book provides an essential argument as to why contemporary organizations need to change and offers practical guidance on how to overcome the waves, while helping your organization to thrive in this new era of management.

This book will appeal to leaders, as well as those involved in human resource management and organizational change.

Luca Solari is a Professor of Organization Theory and Human Resource Management at the University of Milan and Professor of Human Resources in the Faculty of MIP School of Management in Milan for the MBA program. He presently acts as Advisor to EY (former Ernst & Young) People Advisory Services to promote innovation in management and people management. Luca has extensive experience in design and delivery of Corporate Executive training programs, and after a long career as a Strategic Consultant in Organization and HRM, he presently acts as corporate sense maker, blogger, and social media experimenter, investigating the future of work and the future of productivity. Luca's academic work comprises strategy, organizational design issues, and human resource management strategies and practices, with a vast array of research and strategic consulting experience in different industries ranging from service to manufacturing. Luca holds a PhD in Organization and Management Theory.

Freedom Management

How leaders can stay afloat in
the sea of social connections

Luca Solari

Routledge
Taylor & Francis Group

LONDON AND NEW YORK

First published 2017
by Routledge
2 Park Square, Milton Park, Abingdon, Oxon OX14 4RN

and by Routledge
711 Third Avenue, New York, NY 10017

First issued in paperback 2018

Routledge is an imprint of the Taylor & Francis Group, an informa business

British Library Cataloguing in Publication Data
A catalogue record for this book is available from the British Library

Library of Congress Cataloging in Publication Data
Names: Solari, Luca (Professor of management), author.
Title: Freedom management: how leaders can stay afloat in the sea of social connections/Luca Solari.
Description: Abingdon, Oxon; New York, NY: Routledge, 2017.
Identifiers: LCCN 2016011433 | ISBN 9781315583143 (ebook)
Subjects: LCSH: Organizational behavior. | Organizational effectiveness. | Management. | Leadership.
Classification: LCC HD58.7 .S6743 2017 | DDC 658.4/092—dc23
LC record available at https://lccn.loc.gov/2016011433

ISBN 13: 978–1–138–32023–9 (pbk)
ISBN 13: 978–1–4724–4060–0 (hbk)

Typeset in Bembo
by Keystroke, Station Road, Codsall, Wolverhampton

"Now, in its essence, scientific management involves a complete mental revolution on the part of the workingman engaged in any particular establishment (. . .). And it involves the equally complete mental revolution on the part of those on the management's side (. . .). And without this complete revolution on both sides scientific management does not exist."

(Taylor, 1947: Testimony, p. 27)

Contents

Figures

Tables

1 From order to spontaneity

1.1 The evolution of organizations

Organizations are incredible products of human intelligence. They are capable of endeavors which are hard even to imagine. Organizations have brought us where we are today. We have established ourselves as the dominant force of change on our planet, and despite the contradictions and possibly dangerous consequences of this, organizations have made us able to reverse trends and counter unwanted consequences of our activities.

The International Space Station (ISS) organization has combined the efforts of the space agencies of the United States, Russia, Europe, Japan, Canada, and many others to explore life outside the comfort of our planet, creating one of the most complex and ambitious organizations ever. In research, CERN, the European Organization for Nuclear Research, combines the efforts of 21 countries to promote our understanding of the basic building blocks of matter. This is an exemplary organization, where no country is in charge of the program, but all researchers work as a community, and member states are represented in a governing council which operates on informed consensus with the help of independent expert committees. And space is now open to private initiative and private organizations as well. SpaceX is a private company which operates rockets and space transport to the ISS, while seeking to develop a way to make space travel affordable for everybody.

All of this would not be possible if we had not been able at some time in our evolution to design ways to combine our efforts to accomplish the impossible. This was when the very idea of organization was born. Chester Barnard (1938) made a clear statement on the relationship between our ability to organize and our evolution, identifying in organizations the most advanced means to improve cooperation beyond the limits of existing social institutions. I have always been impressed by the vivid description of organizations as the furthest step in human evolution, and this is precisely why, as will become clear in this book, I consider them to be magnificent human achievements.

Hence this book is about organizations, and I thought it important to state what I think of them before criticizing how they have remained more or less unchanged for too many years. I have sought to convey the awe with which I see them operating in the background of our everyday lives. I cannot but be grateful to how organizing has allowed us to progress to what we are today. It is not that I think organizations are only for good. We have had, and probably will have, many examples of how the magic of organizations can be turned into forms of oppression and violence against other human beings.

The reason for this is that as soon as we start organizing, we create the conditions under which we can lose control of organizations and let them evolve as instruments that are under the control of the few, or even worse self-controlled by their own procedures. In a sense, when we organize, we run the risk of losing the power of individual action and initiative, which become subject to the rules, procedures, and goals of the organization.

We are born into believing that the only legitimate way to live together is to follow prescriptions that come from organized bodies of our society. At school we learn what is expected of us and how to behave accordingly. To be sure, in recent times the issue of human development has come under close scrutiny, and education systems are giving way to looser and more autonomous paths to self-development.

Given these limitations, the major question that has accompanied me in twenty years of research is this: how can we use these marvelous instruments while promoting the value of individual liberty? How can we reap the advantages of these elaborate forms of collaboration without converting them into institutions that exert so many constraints on our desires and ambitions?

Throughout my career, I have searched for an answer, first in evolutionary theories, trying to understand how organizations come about, how they evolve, and eventually disband and disappear. I thought that the life cycle of organizations might tell me something about the fact that, as Barnard (1938) stated, collaboration is very difficult to attain, but more importantly to maintain over time. Understanding what brings about organizations, how they unfold during their existence, and how they finally die, might be a way to understand. What I learned left me puzzled. I learned that many of these processes are out of the control of managers, and interestingly that there are times when it is precisely the belief by managers that they can reverse the future of the organization that leads them to failure. I have seen this happen in many different industries, and at many different times in the history of modern business. It was thus that mass beer producers in the USA were cornered by the sudden emergence of smaller microbreweries and brewpubs, or that dominant players could be easily outsmarted by emerging organizations in many other industries, like, for example, the immensely competitive mobile phone arena. It is not that managers at these companies were completely unaware of the oncoming risks or that they failed to react. They simply appeared unable to do anything to rethink their way of doing business. It appeared as if human agency, as it is defined in organizational sociology, did not suffice to manage organizations at times of change. Something made them so inert that they were unable to fight for their survival in the competitive arena. I confess that this made me much more skeptical on the hype surrounding powerful and visible management public figures. I am not so doubtful as to think managers cannot have an impact, and this book clearly states that they can, but I point out that we should not think of them as invincible. My perspective is that more humility and understatement might lead them to a more successful outcome.

Accordingly, while I appreciated the perception that some of these processes are beyond the control of the few in charge, I was dissatisfied because it appeared that no human actor could have any impact on the events being analyzed. Something was missing, as if a famous picture like Edvard Munch's *Scream* lacked the key element of the shouting soul.

And that is exactly when I decided to investigate how organizations shape their relationships with individuals. Another ten years followed, as I tried to understand management and more specifically human resource management, reflecting on the connections between the organizational level and the broader societal level. My research was heavily influenced by my many encounters with HR professionals at very different companies and levels, as well as with many employees who attended training sessions or meetings during consultation projects.

Among the different experiences, one stands out. I spent several years consulting and training at a large Italian telecommunication company. The company enjoyed an excellent reputation on the job market because of its lavish compensation packages, as well as the smartness and competence of its employees, which was recognized on the job market. With no need to engage in formal employee branding (at least for the first ten years or so of its existence), the company was able to attract the best and the brightest. This was of particular impact at top management levels and within the HR function. Many top managers were former high-profile consultants from the Big Three, i.e. Bain, BCG, and McKinsey (strictly in alphabetical order!). The HR function was considered the place to learn what it meant to be a senior HR manager. I had an enjoyable time with them because smart people are always good to talk to and even more to work with and learn from. However, from the outset, I was fascinated by a semi-religious belief in performance management and calibration. The company had inherited the extreme performance culture of the consulting organizations that its top managers came from, and this had translated into an application of the GE approach to performance management, albeit affected by the limits imposed by Italian labor law. When people reached the time of year when performance management was approaching its final stage (evaluation and calibration), everybody was obsessed with mixed feelings. Some dreamed of being promoted or recognized; others feared a less than positive feedback; a handful courageously walked around as if they were DOA (which stands for "dead on arrival," the term used for patients who are clinically dead upon the arrival of professional medical assistance – Wikipedia). The organization was completely absorbed by the anxiety connected with performance management, and everybody was feverish. What puzzled me was that few if any explicitly stated what most of them thought: the process had become a ritual, not a rational and technical tool. Once again, the power of the collective mood of the organization was stronger than individuals. Many of them recognized that their reactions to the performance management process could be considered irrational; but they were still part of that culture and organization, and felt that they had to comply. Individuals were trapped in their organization.

In my search for an answer to how to help people enjoy more liberty in organizations, I soon came to realize that the same issues in the relationship between the individual and the organization could be translated into the sociological analysis of society, and into the search for a solution to the paradox of human agency. In fact, fellow sociologists had been struggling with the need to understand how society appears at any time as a set of defined and structured institutions (which encompass a variety of elements like habits, rituals, role systems, processes, laws, organizations, etc.), while human beings can still be actors, which means that they can promote and enact change. The interplay between organization and individuals could be seen as a specific case of a broader problem. However, the different solutions to this problem still pointed to the dominance of collective institutions over individuals. Human action is always limited by powerful factors which appear to be out of reach. It is as if the blessing of being able to create powerful societal structures as a way to thrive comes with the curse of being somehow subject to their unintended consequences in terms of how they restrict our freedom. If we adopt this perspective, the problem of change in organizations can be interpreted as a conflict between a deliberate plan by human actors and the web of resistance that is embedded in any existing organization by virtue of the structure of roles and the nexus of relations among its members.

I began to investigate the possibility of conceiving organizations as means to allow freedom to flourish, and I started conceiving of them as powerful systems designed to limit that freedom. I still could not completely believe that there was no alternative or that it is impossible to design a different kind of organization.

When I finally thought of this book, it was as if every piece of the puzzle finally found its place, helping me to define the framework on which it rests. My experiences as a researcher and a practitioner were finally converging into a clear perspective on organization.

Evolutionary theories had brought to me the idea that despite all the efforts to impede it, change is happening. I am a firm believer in change, constant change as continuous testing of our limits. Despite the fact that we experience many of our organizations as stable, they thrive with the changes which originate from the irrepressible desire of humans to experiment in different ways with their lives. The fact that change is occurring notwithstanding all the limits imposed by organizations testifies to the importance of individual and human action. While it is reasonable to assume that some changes are consequences of external factors (for example, the drought in California during the summer of 2015, which induced decreased water consumption and identification of possible new sources of water), what I mean is that the core of change is action by individuals and groups. It is only through successive and interconnected choices made by individuals that change comes about. At times, such change may be short-lived and without any real impact on the overall organization; but at other times it will diffuse, become viral, and lead to transformation. This makes me think of how organizations impose barriers and boundaries on our experimentation for the sake of accountability and reliability. Because our actions can have important consequences, organizations are designed in a way that makes it possible to understand who did what so that someone can be held accountable for the impact of their action. Moreover, many processes are repeated in time, and organizations come to be designed in order to ensure reliability, which is the ability to reproduce exactly the same set of actions when required. Reliability is particularly important in manufacturing when the organization must reproduce the same product exactly as it has been designed. In a sense, organizations exist to make change difficult, as a consequence of a model where reproduction is the key competitive factor. In doing so, though, organizations limit innovation and change, and promote inertia. Despite the difficulty, individuals keep changing, and they try to escape from the normalizing and standardizing impact of organizational processes and procedures. At very specific times, however, some of these changes may be considered necessary by the organization and allowed to be implemented or at least tested; or they may simply be so powerful that they emerge notwithstanding any limits imposed on them. Instead, many other, potentially useful, changes will disappear without trace.

From my experience with organizations and people, I believe that action is rooted in our existence, and that it is what defines us as a species. It can be prevented only by setting limits on what we can or cannot experiment with. We have designed organizations to achieve ambitious goals, but there are times when these collective endeavors exert a powerful influence against our desire to do things differently. When this happens, we find ourselves in a struggle between our nature and the necessity to comply with the organizational system. This is a constant struggle from one battle to the next. Eventually, some people give up. It is not that they do not want to change; rather, they accept that they cannot do so within the organization for which they work and look elsewhere for ways to satisfy their basic need for change. Others persevere, or they may even take the lead in pushing organizations into change. The interplay between the human desire for change and resistance by organizations is so complex that I further believe that there is no single path to the future, that there is no hidden project for us, and that there is nobody who can forecast exactly what will happen.

Only experimentation and conscious action can take us in random walks toward the future through which we can find effective routes for future action. This means that in regard to designing our future, I adopt a strictly evolutionary approach whereby we need to promote as many alternatives as possible, test them, learn from the results, and then move on with constant attention to challenging assumptions which worked in the past to verify whether they can still work in the present. The problem is that all these processes occur within a context defined by organizations that have been explicitly designed to limit the evolutionary process that I have described. As a consequence, we experience much less change and experimentation than we could; more importantly we sacrifice so much human talent and innovation on the altar of reliability and accountability.

In conclusion, in the debate on structure (social systems and institutions) versus human agency, I side with human agency, and I maintain that every structure should be considered as a partial equilibrium that tries to reinforce itself, but which we need to keep under control through the constant production of change. If we are really entering what popular videos online define as an exponential world, we need to completely reshape how we organize collective action.

1.2 A theoretical framework

Whilst the purpose of this book is to describe a paradigm shift in how we conceive and design organizations, its roots are firmly in a very specific conception of reality. The reason why existing ways of organizing will not work is precisely because they are rooted in a framework of reality which will no longer be effective. The existing framework favors the ability of societal structure to institutionalize practices.

We can see traces of this in the creation of the concept of "nation," which despite our perception is relatively recent in the time scale of humanity. Historians vary in where they locate its birth, but many converge around the seventeenth century. The concept of "nation" was reinforced by the creation of institutions that would constitute it in practice (organizations, laws, procedures, etc.). Nations could not be born without the creation of institutions that served the purpose of reinforcing the new order and limiting the liberty of individuals with regard to what they could or could not do given their belonging to a specific nation.

This example illustrates the fact that organizations as institutions tend to exert influence on individual behaviors, making them predictable and more standardized. The need to increase the predictability of social encounters has been a key driver of the development of modern societies. This has required a great deal of effort to impose the power of institutions on individuals. We can think of the advantages of the creation of public education systems in order to standardize the knowledge that any citizen should possess. However, we should not forget that this had the consequence of an implicit reduction in the ability to conceive knowledge absorption as an individually-guided process. The price paid has been the reduction of heterogeneity and individuality in complex modern societies. Individuals have disappeared, being replaced by their classification into collectives relevant to the whole of society.

Organizations have reflected the same processes. Whereas at the end of the nineteenth century, Panhard & Levassor, the largest manufacturer of automobiles in France, resembled more a collection of craft workshops than a factory, the advent of the large, integrated factory at Ford changed our idea of organization forever. Whilst at Panhard & Levassor, individual competence was a key success factor, at Ford credit was given to the system for the ability to consistently produce the successful Model T. Hence workers disappeared as individuals to become parts of a process, and a category, connected to the phase in the process where they would be employed.

Figure 1.1 provides a description of this approach to organizations. It all starts from the formal design of how the system should behave. The designer defines a prescribed order aimed at coordinating collective action. This prescribed order relies on standardization of all the elements (roles, actions, procedures, component parts, etc.), and on compliance by all actors involved in the organization. The reality of the organization provides the basis for a constant process of feedback intended to identify gaps between the prescribed order and what has happened in reality. The gaps are the basis for new design in a never-ending cycle aimed at total control over what happens.

The description of this model represents a clear dominance of design over freedom, organization over the individual. What would happen if we were

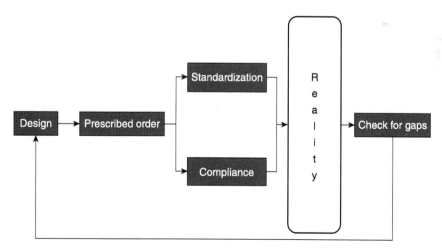

Figure 1.1 The traditional view of organizations

to reverse the assumption and put human action at the origin of any changes in organizations? In this case, order would be the consequence not of an act of design, but of the emergence of spontaneous order among participants in an organization (or in a social system). Individual freedom would interact with this order, enriching it by virtue of human initiative and human variety. The interplay among different actors would shape reality and create new and different forms of spontaneous order, which would induce the cycle to start over and over again.

However, in order to do so, human actors need to be free to express themselves, and release themselves from the constraints of the levels of order to which they are subject because they live in a structured society and operate in a formalized organization. It is for this reason that freedom is the cornerstone of my model.

The existence of freedom to act promotes initiative by actors, which is action directed toward reality; at the same time, freedom to express oneself promotes variety, which is heterogeneity in terms of ideas, intentions, beliefs, goals, etc. The interplay between initiative and variety is confronted with reality, and through cycles of actions and interactions produces spontaneous order. Although represented in linear form, it is clearly an ongoing cycle of evolution driven by the common evolutionary engine of variation-selection-reproduction.

This is my framework for the constitution of organizations (Figure 1.2). I deliberately avoid using the term "design" because I do not think that we are talking about design here. Rather, I am arguing for a "dedesign" (a neologism that follows the idea of degrowth, a descaling of growth) by virtue of which we deliberately reduce the areas of organizational life which are designed.

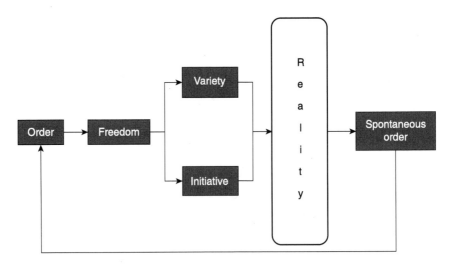

Figure 1.2 The origins of spontaneous order in organizations

On this basis, the book describes how organizational design and management need to be reconsidered to promote freedom, initiative, and variety. This requires controlling the processes through which order (in the form of control and structure) inhibits change, while at the same time promoting initiative by individuals and variety in the composition and pattern of relations among individuals within organizations.

In the following two sections of this first chapter, I explore the theoretical foundations of my approach. Although they represent an integral part of my book, readers not at ease with theorizing can easily jump to the next chapter and maybe return later to clarify the bigger picture of this book, which is about managing organizations differently, but at the same time about thinking them differently.

1.3 I am a phenomenologist

> Now, in its essence, scientific management involves a complete mental revolution on the part of the workingman engaged in any particular establishment. . . . And it involves the equally complete mental revolution on the part of those on the management's side . . . .And without this complete revolution on both sides scientific management does not exist.
>
> (Taylor, 1947: Testimony, p. 27)

As Frederick Winslow Taylor discussed scientific management before the Special House Committee in the winter of 1912, he acknowledged a simple fact: organizations and ways of organizing do not exist if people do not change their minds and attitudes. We can debate as to how this might happen, whether it is a result of self-interest and rational evaluation, a spontaneous mental revolution, an act of discretion or an emotional response, but we cannot neglect this simple fact. Although the process by which this change occurs could help managers to understand how to promote specific change initiatives, I am now interested in directing attention to the link between organizing and world views. In an approach symmetrical to Frederick Winslow Taylor's, also the contrary is true: when people change their minds and attitudes, organizations never dreamt of can be created. The interplay between environment and organizational forms is a centerpiece of the open system view of organizations popularized by many different theories.

Organizations are born and thrive at a specific point in space and time, and they rely on resources which are available in that place and at that time. Stinchcombe (1965) proposed using the concept of available social technology, which is described as a source of imprinting. Available social technology determines the resources that are available to the creator of an organization encompassing many different characteristics like technology, economy, power and social structure, and communication infrastructures, that is, all the accepted ways of interacting within a social system. While we can think of resources in traditional terms as physical resources in the form of materials or money, equally important are intangible resources. Among intangible resources we can include also legitimacy and acceptance of a specific form of organizing, which directs our attention to cognitive resources. Taylor's statement tells us exactly this: the emergence of a new form of organization requires a cognitive revolution.

And this is precisely the point that I want to make because, as I have stated, I do not want to focus on the pattern of interaction between the external environment and organizations, which has received enough attention throughout the evolution of organizational theory. Instead, I intend to establish a clear link between human cognition and the emergence of organizational forms. In my view, organizational forms are phenomena, which means observable social aggregates of which we make sense in our daily interactions with them. As artifacts of human action, they are even more important because they derive from our cognition, in the act of constituting them, and then assume a meaning according to how we experience them.

I am aware that the previous two sentences may be obscure to some readers. However, they express my theoretical perspective, and even more precisely my view of the world as a researcher, technically my epistemology.

It is rather uncommon for a management book, particularly one that does not target solely researchers and theorists, to state from the outset adherence to a specific view of science, in my case phenomenology. However, it is my belief that authors should always declare where they stand in order to avoid being misinterpreted, or even worse misunderstood. All the more so when they propose views of how managers should organize, which in turn will have an impact on employees, managers, and customers. This is particularly important because I stand where few management experts can be found: in direct lineage with a tradition which has its roots in the work by Husserl (1970), a German philosopher who has profoundly influenced social scientists like Max Weber and Frederick von Hayek to whom I will pay many tributes in this book. I maintain that this important tradition of research in social sciences has been neglected in favor of a widespread, and seldom declared, adoption of a naïve positive approach to organizations, with few exceptions (notably Karl Weick, 1995).

So what does it mean to be a phenomenologist who considers the evolution and change of organizations and management?

First, phenomenology studies phenomena, which are things as they appear to us in our experience of the world, as well as the meanings of those same things in our experience as we live through them. From this perspective, the study of organizational forms is not a mere description of how they appear, nor a rationalization of how they should be. Rather, as said above, it is an inquiry into how people experience organizational forms and make sense of them. Central to this is the recognition that which organizational forms will emerge in the future is rooted in how people experience them today as part of the many experiences that they have in their personal lives. As Taylor clearly recognized, there can be no organizational form or management approach without a change of mind. Rigorous research in management cannot be restricted to describing and analyzing what has happened; rather, it needs to concentrate also on what could happen on the basis of a method of inquiry into intentions. Phenomena are inherently dynamic because they are based on the interaction between us and the world that we see. None of these interactions can ever be considered neutral because they constitute the basis for a change in our perception of any external object that we observe. Organizations are even less neutral because they are essentially continuous flows of interconnected actions which require an observer to be made sense of.

Second, phenomenology directs our attention as management researchers to intentionality or *aboutness*. How we experience things is always connected to the intentions that we have in concentrating on them. This is a very delicate and important point. Most management research tends to overlook the fact that management approaches and practices are given a meaning by individuals through a process which is directed at them by intentions: that is, the concepts, ideas, values, thoughts, and images that we possess. Any inquiry into the viability of organizational forms must recognize the centrality of the views of all the individuals connected to their emergence. In a phenomeno-logical perspective, organizations can be viewed differently according to the standpoint of the observer. At the same time, if the perspective changes, so will the interpretation and experience of the organization by its viewer.

Third, a particular version of phenomenology, which is the one derived from Alfred Schutz's work (Schutz, 1970), allows us to identify two drivers of action. One is the *because motive*, which represents the historical factors that led to the undertaking of an action; the other is the *in-order-to motive*, which reflects an act of projection into the future to imagine the consequence of the intended action. Interestingly, most research on organization and management adopts a framework whereby an attempt is made to identify the classic cause-effect relation which is at the roots of positive science and the hard sciences. Although I consider this important, I consider as equally important the ability to inquire into the reasons and intentions for action. While Max Weber (2010) is not considered a phenomenologist, because of his reliance on the idea that we can identify ideal types on the basis of our experience of things, the phenomenological approach shares his view that any understanding of social and economic systems requires understanding of the actions of actors, and how they choose among several possible alter-natives. It appears clear, I hope, that phenomenology sets the human actor at the center of what happens and assigns to him/her the ability to project actions into the future on the basis of intentionality.

In conclusion, a phenomenological alternative to the analysis of organ-izations and management departs from the existing literature in three ways:

1. It concentrates on how actors' beliefs affect the emergence of viable forms.
2. It assigns a role to intentions, projects, and desires.
3. It attempts to provide a view of what can happen, rather than describing what has happened.

1.4 I am inspired by classic liberalism

Management theorists seem to follow the advice of Max Weber, who argued that social scientists should be observers and not militants. In reality, what happens is that the ideological point of view is left implicit. The books that pay some attention to making this explicit are those that intend to criticize the predominant normative (i.e. that defines what should be done in absolute terms) and functional (i.e. that analyzes management practices in terms of their immediate consequences and functions) approach of mainstream management literature.

Given that my point of view is rather unique in this context, I think it important to emphasize that besides being a phenomenologist, I am deeply influenced in my interpretation of reality and organizations by classic liberalism. As the reader progresses through this book, s/he will notice that the foundation of my ideas is the firm belief in the overarching value of liberty as the essential root of human society.

As a phenomenologist, I know that how we direct our attention to things in the external world has much to do with how we have framed our intentions. Moreover, I recognize that individuals experience things through different intentions, and that the belief that the things which we observe (and even more concepts, ideas, and values) are objective is nothing but naïve. However, I recognize that through inter-subjectivity (i.e. the creation of a somewhat shared understanding of reality) individuals can reach consensus and agreement on how to experience the world outside, but that the liberty of an individual to experience his/her own world is somehow an essential and undisputable value which is far more important than consensus and agreement.

I consider any inter-subjective agreement, not as a stable institutionalization of reality to which people will have to adapt (as in social constructionist interpretations of reality), but as a step in the process of consciousness. Individuals interact with an ever-changing reality and reach localized and temporary agreements on how to interpret it and act accordingly. However, the power of individual action constantly pushes toward novel interpretations of reality which further extend the boundaries of our knowledge domain. The same processes that are experienced by people in their interaction with the external world and among themselves occur within organizations. Caught in a never-ending challenge to improve our understanding of reality and improve how our organizations operate, the adoption of localized and temporary agreements in the form of spontaneous orders can give way to novel ideas and interpretations of reality. In order to take advantage of this process, therefore, organizations and institutions should concentrate on allowing heterogeneous interpretations of reality, granting all individuals the maximum amount of freedom. Unfortunately, as I have shown in the previous sections, this is not the most common interpretation of the role of institutions and organizations, which are usually focused on maintaining accountability and reliability, thereby limiting exploration and change.

The importance that I assign to individual action and freedom to act illustrates the other theoretical cornerstone of this book. While my approach is phenomenological, I consider organizations through the lenses of another perspective, which appears rather neglected in management despite its profound impact on economics: classic liberalism (Hayek, 1978). It is no coincidence that both Ludwig von Mises and Frederick von Hayek, two of the founding fathers of the Austrian School of liberalism, were deeply influenced by (and in turn influenced) phenomenology, as testified by their close friendship with Schutz (Augier, 1999) who participated in many workshops and research meetings in Vienna. In fact, both perspectives share the intent to assign individuals an important role in the social realm.

Classic liberalism is a political philosophy based on the absolute value of liberty, which is traditionally connected to the earlier formulation of the notion by the English philosopher John Locke. Hayek defined liberty as "the state in which a man is not subject to coercion by the arbitrary will of another or others" (Hayek, 1978: 11). This idea of liberty in turn constitutes the basis for asserting the role of spontaneous order in the definition of social systems. Given that all individuals strive to defend their liberty, but acknowledge the advantage of creating some shared understanding of the reality to which they refer, human societies have developed means to order interactions which were not designed by any central authority but emerged spontaneously through years of encounters and experimentations. Other than limiting an individual's liberty, the emerging spontaneous order maximizes the collective gains with no need of design or enforcement. Hayek counterposed spontaneous order to designed order mostly in the form of state-centered ways to govern the economic system. Given the scale of the allocation problem to be faced, he contended that no central authority can possess enough knowledge to solve this problem optimally, and markets have emerged because they seem able to do so effortlessly and with no direct intervention.

Hayek is considered the key author to comprehend the link between classic liberalism and modern liberalism (Petsoulas, 2013). A central tenet of Hayek's liberalism is the idea of spontaneous order, by virtue of which all institutions can be interpreted as the outcome of "unintended and unforeseen spontaneous coordination of a multiplicity of actions by self-interested individuals" (Petsoulas, 2013: 2). According to Hayek, the complexity of coordinating social systems impedes the use of planned and designed institutions. Instead of reverting to planning, institutions rely substantially on cultural evolution, which is a process analogous to natural evolution whereby rules emerge to respond to the environment through variation, and are subsequently subject to selection.

Central to Hayek's view of society is his assumption on how individuals experience reality. The view that he holds is connected with phenomenology and hermeneutics (DiIorio, 2013) because of his concept of a circular causality between perception and memory in which memory affects how we perceive the world, but at the very same time affects our memory of the world through constant surprise. Once again, this concept lies at the roots of why Hayek does not believe in centralization. In fact, apart from problems connected with the distributed knowledge of the circumstances, centralization cannot occur effectively because individuals will experience and interpret those circumstances on the basis of different presuppositions which are constantly changing and evolving.

It is unfortunate that management theorists have not been familiar with Hayek's criticism of centralization, because it appears clear that attempts to promote entrepreneurship and empowerment within established organizations will fail unless they are made consistent with an organizational design that gets rid of any forms of centralization and control.

Another key tenet of liberalism is its proposal of a new social science, praxeology, which was introduced by Mises and further discussed within the Austrian School (Selgin, 1988; Rothbard, 1976). In developing praxeology, Mises extended the notion of purposefulness, and Weber's notion of an entirely value-free science of human action, to derive entire sets of propositions on human action.

Praxeology is a view of human nature based on action. In fact, its core element is the axiom of action based on observation of the connection between being human and acting purposefully to achieve goals. In its original formulation, praxeology is a science based on the deductive implications stemming from the axiom of action. It is important to note that "axiom" has a completely different meaning from "postulate." An axiom is a statement or proposition that is regarded as being established, accepted, or self-evidently true, while a postulate is something suggested or assumed as true as the basis for reasoning, discussion, or belief. Praxeology does not evaluate the appropriateness of actions or the choice of means to achieve ends; it "asserts that the individual actor adopts goals and believes, whether erroneously or correctly, that he can arrive at them by the employment of certain means" (Rothbard, 1976: 59).

An in-depth analysis of praxeology would fall outside the scope of this book. However, as Selgin (1988) points out, it has evolved into a highly contested terrain. One of the key issues is the possibility of determining how other actors will behave in the future, which has led to definition of the future as kaleidic, that is, "dominated by patternless change" (Selgin, 1988: 20).

In the book, I will refer to praxeology when discussing the reasons why we cannot but expect individuals to demand transformational change in how we organize collective action. The book is in fact based on the consideration of profound changes in societal values which will in turn influence goals that actors will set themselves, and in this process require organizations to change accordingly lest they be wiped out.

In conclusion, extending liberalism to the analysis of organizations and management means that in this book I will:

1. concentrate on the key role that liberty plays also within organizations,
2. consider individual choices on the basis of praxeology, and
3. illustrate how spontaneous order can be more effective than order obtained through planning and controlling.

1.5 Concluding remarks

The inspiration that I draw from phenomenology and classic liberalism frames how I interpret management and research on management and organization. Like any social science, management would benefit greatly from more clarity on which epistemology researchers adopt. Unfortunately, attention to this basic tenet of research has decreased in parallel with the unprecedented spread of management literature, which appears to be implicitly biased toward a positivistic and normative description of organizations.

The revitalization of phenomenology and classic liberalism opens a window of opportunity that I believe better captures what organizations and workers are currently experiencing, particularly where external socio-economic, and political conditions allow them to express their intentions fully.

The previous paragraphs have provided a general description of these approaches to social sciences, but I think it is useful to summarize the key tenets of my approach.

First, in this book I contend that spontaneous order is superior in dealing with complex collective problem-solving to any form of hierarchy and centralized control also within organizations and not only in economic systems. Although hierarchy has contributed greatly to the advancement of human societies, the evolution of markets and the emergence of the network society (Castells, 1996) are pushing it to its limits. The resilience of this form of social technology, however, is closely connected to the fact that it has shaped our society, and notably the power relations within it. Despite these limits, innovative organizations are taking advantage of the fact that novel social technologies are emerging as a consequence of the dramatic reduction of perceived distances in both time and space made possible by the widespread use of internet-based technologies. Instead of evaluating the trade-off between work and free time as commonly considered in economic models of work relations, I contend that people are moving toward considering the trade-off between liberty and constraint; in fact, work and free time will not differ much once people are allowed to act freely in each of the two domains.

Second, I subscribe to the idea that innovation in organization and management is a product of in-order-to motives, which are the projects, ideas, endeavors, and desires of individual actors. The rapidity with which new organizations will emerge is directly connected to the increase in freedom of action by those very same actors in the larger society, but also within the boundaries of existing organizations. The fact that in-order-to motives are seldom recognized in current research is a consequence of the limits of a positivistic epistemology, which is so concentrated on cause-effect relations that it completely underestimates the importance of (apparently) unimaginable and (probably) unpredictable actions. As a phenomenologist, whilst I recognize that it is difficult to predict if and when something will happen, I defend the idea that a researcher can help envision possible futures on the basis of the analysis of intentionality. The methodology that I apply is consistent with praxeology, whereby I derive consequences for organizations from the idea that actors will follow paths of purposeful action, directed toward goals, by choosing means and technologies.

Third, I recognize that the changes ahead will meet much resistance because, as with the emergence of scientific management, they will require a profound change, a mental revolution, which will alter power relations and the very structure of society. From this perspective, in preparing this book I have found it very useful to critically review the debate on the future of society, which is rich with elements for thoughtful managers (see for example: Beck, 1992; Castells, 1996; Bauman, 2000; Sennett, 2000).

Quite interestingly, the most notable examples of innovation in management which are popularized by the press are emerging in the vicinity of places which used to be marginal for traditional big business, like universities (for example, Stanford in Silicon Valley) or social movements (for example, the Open Source movement behind Linux). It is at the periphery of the large, established, traditional hierarchies that there is enough opportunity for change, and enough rebelliousness, to promote discontinuity. Interestingly, many of these examples do not relate to traditional critical and radical movements, organized for class or power struggles, but to the emergence of a form of libertarianism which has come to characterize profoundly, for example, Silicon Valley, and more generally entrepreneurs in the start-up era. Notably, the important link between a shift in societal values and the emergence of new organizational forms, though popularized by the media, has not generated scholarly reflection.

My book attempts to provide a grounding for redefinition of how organizations should be designed along the lines of the evolving nature of available social technology, which is in turn prompted by the ongoing process of liberation of the individual which has roots in Renaissance humanism (Simmel, 1972), and by the powerful innovation of social and collaborative technologies that we can employ in our everyday lives.

The following chapters will guide the reader through discovery of how profound the changes will be, and how they are anticipated by many processes which are occurring right now.

2 Toward a different social order

The interplay between institutions and society is a key tenet in social sciences. In fact, while institutions cannot but be products of social systems and individual actors, the latter are influenced by institutions. The circularity of this self-evident process poses several problems as to how institutions emerge, develop, and are eventually superseded by novel ones.

Organizations are institutions because they are "a complex of positions, roles, norms and values lodged in particular types of social structures and organising relatively stable patterns of human activity with respect to fundamental problems in producing life-sustaining resources, in reproducing individuals, and in sustaining viable societal structures within a given environment" (Turner, 1997: 6). As institutions, business organizations are subject to the same processes of change and evolution which take place between individual actors and social institutions.

The interplay between individual actors and social institutions allows for the emergence of tensions between the two, as for example when social movements arise to oppose existing institutions or seek to modify or alter the way in which they are designed or operate, and eventually promote new institutions. An interesting example for business organizations is the history of the TQM (Total Quality Management) movement described by Rao et al. (2000), who illustrate how the social movement toward a different conception of quality had to develop its own institutions and organizations to disseminate its approach in American business. Some institutional changes are more similar to a slow, continuous drift that does not let tensions emerge for long periods of time; others erupt as severe social confrontations and revolts.

In business terms, the resilience of large corporations may not be enough to shield them from the consequences of such changes. Nokia, which was long the dominant player in the handset industry, could not cope with changes introduced through smartphone design by players like Apple and Samsung, and ended up being acquired by Microsoft. Shell had to engage in a long battle over its reputation following its support for military operations against the Ogoni ethnic group in Nigeria which resulted in extreme violations of human rights.

These are two of the many examples of the consequences that business organizations suffer from their inability to incorporate changes occurring in the external environment. However, they are still minor examples of change pressures if compared to those that await companies in the near future as a consequence of a broader shift in societal values comparable only to the one that brought about the modern corporation in the twentieth century.

The challenges that lie ahead are systemic in nature because they affect the values which are the foundations of existing organizations. These challenges stem from two different but interdependent processes taking place at the individual and societal level. At the individual level, it is the search by individuals to fulfill three universal basic needs, which have long been overlooked by business organizations, to create an important threat to existing organizations. At the societal level, it is the emergence of three dominant values which span across societies and generations despite the resurgence of extreme traditional views of society in the wake of religious movements in some areas across the globe.

To paraphrase Henry Mintzberg and his power of the number five, it seems that we witness the power of the number three: three universal basic needs and three social values at the roots of a dramatic change that faces institutions, and among them, business organizations.

2.1 Our search for the three universal basic needs: autonomy, relatedness, and competence

The evolution of organizational forms proceeds towards ever-growing variety in striking analogy with the evolution of life forms, albeit on a shorter time scale, which allows us to be aware of it unlike biological evolution, which operates on longer time scales. This evolution is driven by the conscious actions of individuals, the creators of organizations, and it is a reflection of a more general process that pushes the boundaries of our collective knowledge.

The drive toward knowledge that we experience has been described by various theories. For example, philosophical anthropology relates it to the limits of humans as non-adapted animals that needed to develop technology in order to survive (Gehlen, 1989). In economics, it is commonplace to refer to the idea of creative destruction as a powerful engine of change through entrepreneurial action (Schumpeter, 2013).

However, this drive has roots in our constitution as human beings constantly striving to change our external environment to improve our life conditions. As Gehlen (1989) puts it, Man is an interesting case of a non-adapted animal that needs to develop technology to survive in an hostile environment; once developed, though, technology becomes an instrument that allows Man to occupy all environmental niches because it acts as an extension of the human body.

This drive toward action rests on our characteristics as human beings and responds to this never-ending quest. Many theories have attempted to describe how this happens. Among them, self-determination theory (SDT) (Ryan and Deci, 2000) is an account of how we are shaped that is consistent with a positive view of the individual and his/her liberty. Therefore it is connected to the ideological inspiration of this book, which concentrates on the importance of individual action through liberty. Moreover, it lies at the heart of a profound movement in social sciences aimed at revitalizing the view of human beings. This has used the adjective "positive" as its watchword and was originated by Martin Seligman, who coined the term positive psychology (PP) (Seligman and Csikszentmihalyi, 2000).

The connection between SDT and PP has been made explicit by Ryan himself in a chapter recently published in a book that he edited with Chirkov and Sheldon on human autonomy (Sheldon and Ryan, 2011). According to these authors, SDT "provides a universalist or trans-cultural account of optimal human functioning, based on evolutionary-psychological or adaptationist reasoning" (Sheldon and Ryan, 2011: 33). At the core of SDT lies the assumption that people are born with a propensity toward becoming more self-determined and self-regulated, which accounts for the fact that institutions and organizations which behave in an autonomy-supportive way can help individuals thrive. It is important here to recognize the possible links between SDT and praxeology. In fact, despite their differing intents, the two perspectives both point to the existence of a propensity for action by human beings. While praxeology treats it as an axiom, SDT explores intrinsic motivation as an evolved propensity which is evident in "the inherent tendency to seek out novelty and challenges, to extend and to exercise one's capacities, to explore, and to learn" (Ryan and Deci, 2000: 70). Interestingly, SDT develops an analysis of the conditions which enhance and sustain or diminish and discourage this propensity, adding to the analysis of human action the dimension of the external environment.

According to SDT, individuals who experience personal autonomy, a feeling of competence, and relatedness, enhance their well-being, and this occurs despite cultural differences because it is a constitutive characteristic of all human beings with the same universal appeal as praxeology.

SDT posits that autonomy, competence, and relatedness are the three basic psychological needs which are constitutive of human nature and promote well-being if satisfied.

The need for autonomy is defined as "individuals' inherent desire to feel volitional and to experience a sense of choice and psychological freedom when carrying out an activity" (Broeck et al., 2010: 982). The need for competence is defined as "individuals' inherent desire to feel effective in interacting with the environment" (Broeck et al., 2010: 982). Finally, the need for relatedness is defined as "individuals' inherent propensity to feel connected to others, that is, to be a member of a group, to love and care and be loved and cared for" (Broeck et al., 2010: 982–83). According to

SDT, these needs may be met or hampered in the external context with consequences for individuals' level of intrinsic motivation, and hence for well-being and performance.

It appears logical that the three basic needs should be considered when defining the design of organizations. In fact, because these basic needs are intrinsic to personal growth and fulfillment, individuals will strive to find external contexts where they can develop them fully. At a time when many theories tend to be openly relativist in terms of how local cultures and habits influence individuals, SDT has provided evidence of a universal trend across very different cultures like those of China, the USA, South Korea, Turkey, and Taiwan (Sheldon et al., 2004).

It is striking to see how SDT theory, despite being rooted in a completely different time and perspective, reflects the profound beliefs in individuals and their self-determination which underpin the view of human beings in liberalism and in Schutz's phenomenology. I consider this to be another element of a resurgence of individual determination of social facts after the long dominance of institutions and socialized action. Whilst I acknowledge the many contributions that have derived from this approach, I personally think that study and research on human behavior, and more specifically organization and management, should refocus more on the individual actor. By this I do not intend to subscribe to a solipsistic view of organizations as molded by solitary leaders. Rather, I point to the need to open up the black box of what happens in reality, considering each individual as a point of reference and as a perspective for knowing. With this in mind, it will be easier to escape the traps of (presumed) objective organizational design and narrow the gap between what we design and what really happens in organizations.

Organizations are made by individuals who decide to act in a collaborative way. Although we can trace their behaviors back to self-interest, and rely on incentives to account for this marvel of human cooperation, we cannot ignore the fact that they exhibit individual choice. It is common to hear employees complain about how the organization is imposing constraints on their ideas and actions. This should prompt us to look more carefully into how much space is left for them to express their desires when we have constructed organizational systems which target standardization and control. According to SDT, the way in which we have designed organizations is the very reason why so many companies complain about the low levels of engagement and commitment that employees exhibit. Instead of understanding that the solution is to renounce the idea of controlling them, their behaviors and even their thoughts, managers tend to respond by inflicting even more control on employees. While practitioners tend to attribute the negative consequences of engagement surveys to the lack of credible follow-ups in terms of actions and interventions, I have developed the idea that the drawback of these surveys is that they make people realize how little freedom they have within most modern organizations.

When I consider the powerful impact of the three basic needs portrayed by SDT, the real question concerning how to engage employees to a greater extent is how we should design organizations (and institutions) differently so as to break out of the excess of constraints.

Once again, a visual image that can aid understanding of the power inherent in this liberation can be derived from two iconic videos. The first is the videoclip of *The Wall* by the English band Pink Floyd, which depicts the need to let children experience learning and education in a different way by tearing down the wall of established education. The other video brings together two of my personal icons, George Orwell and Apple. It is the famous television commercial broadcast during the US Super Bowl in 1984 where people rebel against Big Brother. Those powerful images are at the heart of this book, and they demonstrate in an intuitive way how I feel about the need for a dramatic change in organizations. And this change starts from a complete revolution in terms of what values should lie at the roots of organizational design.

2.2 Organizing for autonomy, competence, and relatedness embracing novel values: liberty, cooperation, and sense

Traditional organizational design has not explicitly considered the impact of the three basic psychological needs described by SDT, at least not by bundling them within a unified framework. Whilst the interplay between the human and technical factors has always been a key theme in organizational theory, there is no trace of a theory which has been developed from the standpoint of a truly human value perspective. In fact, even the more closely connected human relations theory is concerned with the interplay between organizational processes and human motivation, adhering to the idea that humans constitute one of the resources that enable organizations to perform. Other established theories tend to treat the human actor as a black box or to deal with the unintended consequences of the submission of individuals to organizational systems. Even the socio-technical approach balances between technical and social factors, assigning the same importance to both.

Interestingly, organizational design is affected by the same over-reliance on systems and constraints that I discuss throughout this book. While organizations are clearly in place as artifacts of humankind, they seem to have taken on a life of their own, imposing constraints which appear to be objective but should rather be considered as self-imposed boundaries on our human action.

Despite the fact that I recognize that the tone of this book may be at the border between research and futurology, I would urge the reader to think of the many profound criticisms of this state of affairs that have appeared in science-fiction novels. I have already mentioned *1984* by George Orwell in the previous section, but many of the same themes on the unresisted defeat of humankind by systems are present in such masterpieces as *Slaughterhouse-Five* or *The Children's Crusade* by Kurt Vonnegut or the many books by Philip K. Dick. The difference that I would like to emphasize is that while science fiction projects these issues into the distant future, mostly with a negative perception of our preparedness to confront them, I think contemporary organizations are already showing signs of their inability to exert control. To continue with the science-fiction analogy, I side more with the human-directed optimism of the *Doctor Who* series than with the dire pessimism of the authors that I have mentioned.

And in fact, organizational research shows signs of concern and points to the need to promote the three basic needs in organizational settings. Indeed, there are sparse traces of each of them in different perspectives on management and organization theory. For example, autonomy has received attention at the micro level in socio-technical theory (Hackman and Oldham, 1976) or in the literature on psychological empowerment (Spreitzer, 1995), and at the macro level in the discussion of the emergence of the M-form organization (Bartlett and Ghoshal, 1993; Ouchi, 1984). Competence is a key element of research on HR management practices (Mansfield, 1996), and a key tenet of one very successful strategy perspective (Prahalad and Hamel, 1990). Relatedness is present in human relations theory, albeit not as a specific term (Mayo, 1949), and to some extent can be connected to the role of cooperation in organizational design, which is a guiding theme in Chester Barnard's study (Barnard, 1938). However, no perspective considers them all or addresses them all as basic principles on how we need to design organizations to improve well-being and performance at the same time. This fact lies at the heart of this book because it signals a gap between what we have come to know about individuals and the dominant ideology that relies mostly on systems to manage complex tasks.

The question becomes that of developing a different approach to organizational design, one that builds upon the three universal needs instead of subjecting them to the constraints of technical systems. In fact, the way that we have looked at organizational design is influenced by the belief that design can never be perfect but results from trade-offs to be taken into account. Interestingly, this has led at least one author (i.e. Robert W. Keidel) to identify a pair of elements in organizational design which reflect two of the universal needs described in SDT. An interesting feature of this author is that he shares with another non-mainstream researcher (Chester Barnard) the fact that he is not an academic but a reflective practitioner, i.e. a practitioner who attempts to convert his experience into theory and ends up becoming a researcher later in his professional life. Autonomy and cooperation appear as elements in Keidel's triangular model for organizational design (Keidel, 1995), which he developed to describe the different approaches to organizational restructuring. Keidel's model interprets organizations as a balance of hierarchical control, individual/unit autonomy, and spontaneous cooperation (Figure 2.1). He relies on the idea that organizations deal with

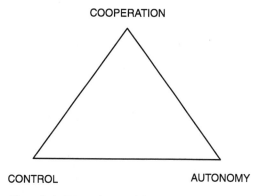

COOPERATION

CONTROL   AUTONOMY

Figure 2.1 Triangular model (Keidel, 1995: p. 18)

conflicting pressures and need to accommodate them. My interpretation of this fact is that organizational design postulates the existence of a pre-defined optimal technical solution which does not take explicit account of human needs and limits. The latter come to be considered only later in the process, and it is for this reason that there arise conflicts related to the constraints imposed on individuals to adhere to the rational design of the technical part of the organizational system.

The rationale behind Keidel's model is that every organization needs to:

- prioritize control, autonomy, and cooperation in order to solve the trade-offs which originate among them;
- integrate the three variables because they are interdependent and necessary;
- focus on each of them at the time when they demand attention.

According to Keidel, organizations struggle to integrate the three axes in a dynamic manner. In fact, while traditional organizational design models and frameworks can be interpreted as rather stable configurations where one of the three axes is largely dominant, the challenge for organizations at present is to strike a balance among them and rapidly readjust to ever-changing priorities. In the past, in fact, we have observed the learning organization model, which clearly favored cooperation over the other dimension, or the M-form, which chose autonomy as its guiding principle, and finally the traditional bureaucratic organization, which relied on control. Each of these different models could be related to very specific external and internal factors which favored one or the other. In this vein, in stable, quite homogeneous environments the bureaucratic organization clearly surpassed the others, while in multiple and heterogeneous environments with rather stable characteristics, the M-form would be dominant; and the learning organization would emerge when the organization operated in a homogenous, but highly volatile environment. Despite their consistency with different external conditions, thorough consideration of the nature of the three basic needs explored in the previous section reveals that these different organizational design models all failed to create a context conducive to intrinsic motivation.

Each of these organizational models represented a solution well suited to adapting the technical system, or core as Thompson (2011) termed it, to the external environment, while they neglected the consequences of this fit for individuals. The lack of concern with the consequences of organizational models for individuals stems from the deep-rooted belief that any organizational solution will always be a sort of trade-off between efficiency and well-being. Rather than taking this for granted within a paradigm for the establishment of society and organization, I believe that we need to reverse this assumption. Organizations are instruments to power human capabilities, but they need to be based on the assumption that human and individual values should be the major constraints on design. If organizations are based on this assumption, then given the flexibility of human capital, they may enhance their ability to be adaptive, and even proactive, with much less effort than today. In fact the constraints imposed by the highly structured organization that derive from technical limits raise a strong challenge against any kind of organizational change. However, while many practitioners tend to attribute the difficulty of organizational change to human resistance, I am convinced that such resistance is only a side-product of the high structuration to which individuals are subject within organizations. If organizations were more flexible and really based on individual freedom, change would probably be experienced as a mere fact of reality, and not as a complex, expensive, difficult process.

Hence while Keidel's model still proposes to operate on trade-offs, now organizations are challenged to embrace all three axes, and to shift their priorities rapidly from one to the other. They can do this only by reversing their perspective as to what design should be. This is because their internal and external constituencies are pressuring them toward a new set of values rooted in the search for the three universal basic needs. Despite the fact that after the first appearance of the individual in society at the end of the Middle Ages, and its reinforcement at the time of the American and French revolutions, collective views on how to organize human actions have taken the lead in society and business, the ongoing process of liberation of the individual is still in action. Society is now ready to take another step forward in this liberation. Organizations and institutions have been built to resist this uncontrollable force, and they still operate on the belief that the normalization and standardization of behaviors are the correct goals. Individuals, however, are developing different views, as shown by the unrest with which they react to organizational and institutional constraints imposed on them. The outburst of innovation that originated from Silicon Valley has spread to many different places in the world. Incubators, business accelerators, shared office spaces for start-ups, and many other places are popping up everywhere, at all latitudes.

They testify to the demise of the large, integrated organization in favor of the entrepreneurial spirit which is rooted in a search for liberty. Leading companies worldwide may have fewer than 100 employees or members, like Uber. One cannot but recognize in this the emergence of the basic needs for autonomy, competence, and relatedness. Incumbent organizations must morph themselves into collectives suited to this new environment. If they do not, they are doomed. It is only a question of time. So I think that if you have a role in your own organization, you should prepare yourself for what is to come.

It is true that this process is not ubiquitous. There are reactions, even extreme and violent ones, in different parts of the world. Individual values seem to be strongly contested in several areas of the Middle East at the time of writing. The resurgence of violent, extremist, religious movements has far-reaching consequences for the everyday lives of people everywhere. However, I consider this to be due to the fact that progress toward a freer humanity has gained momentum. This poses threats to traditional institutions and roles, provoking a violent reaction in some contexts.

Despite the many problems that they have caused, business organizations have played a leading role in this process by conveying new values across borders even into highly controlled and oppressive societies. People in business have led progress toward the creation of a truly global community of individuals sharing ideals while respecting differences. It is thanks to them and the companies to which they belong that individual rights in areas like sexual preferences, gender, religious beliefs, and many other sources of potential diversity are being increasingly recognized and legitimated across the world. One can never be thankful enough to business organizations for these consequences, although they have also come at the expense of much wrongdoing in the exploitation of resources and human labor. For this reason, business organizations should go to great lengths to regain legitimacy, given their many misdemeanors, or even felonies. A central requirement in this process is clearly their ability to establish integrity in their operations at all levels. A driver of such a change would be the ability to rethink all their operations by putting people first in the true sense of the expression. And the only way to put people first is to place liberty at the core of any reorganization of their operations.

Business leaders seem to have recognized the need to reshape their organizations to accommodate a radical shift in values. The evidence is dispersed across different streams of discussion, but it is apparent for example in the discourse on the needs of the new generations at work and in the market, which seem to be different from those of the "baby boomers." Many managers perceive that the levers that they used to use to engage employees are not working properly in engaging employees today. At a time when companies can host up to five different generations of workers, thanks to the increased life span and the better life-conditions at elderly age, diversity in managing is no longer a "nice to have" value in the HR department, but the very core of any people-management capability. And because diversity is hard to classify once and for all, this means that managers need to listen more carefully to what people are looking for, instead of relying on mass models of individual behavior as happened in traditional organizations until a few years ago.

Hence, while individuals are pushing for the satisfaction of their universal needs, society is incorporating new values which reflect at the collective level the individual processes explored in the previous section. And as SDT has done for individual needs, different research in the domain of demography and politics has described what is happening around us.

Inglehart, an American political scientist, has pointed out in his book *The Silent Revolution* (Inglehart, 2015) that societal values are changing rapidly, with an increasing emphasis on values that center on belonging, esteem, and self-realization. According to Inglehart, Western societies are moving toward post-materialism because the emerging generations have been liberated from the constraints of basic acquisitive or materialistic needs. While Inglehart acknowledges the differences among countries, he posits that the changes observed in Western society are part of an overall trend which will affect all countries and communities. As for the challenges for the time being, they are reflected in the still profound differences among countries depicted by the Inglehart-Welzel cultural map of the world (Inglehart and Welzel, 2010). This map projects countries on the basis of their scores in the World Values Survey on two dimensions: traditional versus secular-rational values on the vertical y-axis, and survival versus self-expression values on the horizontal x-axis (Figure 2.2).

The map shows how countries differ in this important respect. As cultures transition from traditional to secular-rational values, they abandon beliefs rooted in religion and superstition and embrace rational and scientific principles. The move from survival to self-expression values, instead, signals the demise of economic and physical security in favor of self-expression, well-being and quality of life. The map reveals countries where the values at the origin of the changes described in this book are already well-established. However, it should be noted that the map does not reflect the cultural values in the business world, where we should expect less heterogeneity than in general societies. Moreover, as Inglehart states, the trend toward a more secular society favoring self-expression is a general shift toward the upper-right corner of the map.

An important consequence of these changes is that organizations must be organized so that they can promote the emerging values if they want to attract and retain people in the future. They already face problems when they operate with a traditional model in the upper-right countries, and they will increasingly find themselves in difficulties.

In order to be able to promote ways of organizing that are respectful of the emerging values, organizations must rethink their basic design principles. In fact, the design principles in use at most organizations are those established

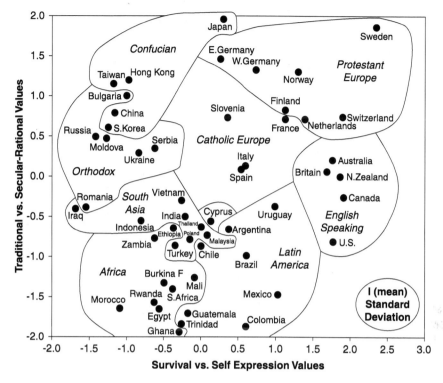

Figure 2.2 The Inglehart-Welzel cultural map of the world (source: Inglehart and Welzel, 2010)

Source: Data from World Values Survey. The oval at the lower right shows the mean size of the standard deviation on each of the two dimensions *within* the 53 societies (the shape is oval because the S.D. on the horizontal axis is larger than on the vertical axis).

at the dawn of industrialization, and they have been only partially adapted to the new landscape of society and business.

My view is that the societal values described by Inglehart point to an important shift of design principles (Table 2.1) in the direction of organization structures and processes which are more conducive to self-expression.

In the design of organizations liberty needs to take the place of control so that members of organizations can feel free to express themselves and

Table 2.1 A shift in design principles

From	To
Control	Liberty
Competition	Cooperation
Task	Sense

increase their ability to satisfy the powerful need for autonomy. Control was a design principle rooted in the need to align human behavior with the requirements of the technical system. In part, this reflected the incomplete development of human capital and human skills at the time of the emergence of modern organizations compared to the amazing advancement in technology, which required standardized work activities. It has also played a role in defining a social structure sufficiently stable to ensure social cohesion. It had an important role at the time when societies were mostly emerging from the lower-left quadrant of the Inglehart-Welzel graph. At a time when decisions should be flexible, and standardization cannot be used to coordinate the majority of valuable relations in organizations, control needs to be abandoned for greater reliance on individuals and their desire to contribute to a collective endeavor. Instead of defining structures of action, design has the role of identifying where liberty and autonomy are limited by existing structures, processes and procedures and actively removing the constraints, to liberate individual action and proactivity.

Competition should give way to cooperation whereby organizational members can find a context that allows them to fulfill their desires for belonging and at the same time self-realization. When modern organizations were conceptualized and created, humanity had the problem of limited resources. In that context, competition among participants allowed only a few to emerge. It created the sense of urgency that was considered necessary to coordinate complex collective action. Competition was a means to align individuals with an organization's goals. In today's organizations, individuals are usually much better educated and prepared; they understand the complexity of the organization more fully; and they can adhere to its goals on the basis of a desire for cooperation. In turn, this responds to the changes in society discussed above, while also powering the ability of organizations to find innovative solutions by leveraging collaborative work.

Finally, organizational design needs to substitute task (a specific role and set of activities to perform, which have been defined and standardized) with sense. By sense I mean the possibility of identifying a direction for individual and collective action, and organizing oneself, one's activities, and one's local organization to fulfill the search for a solution to relevant problems. The quest for meaning in one's work is an important issue in contemporary organizations. Whilst it has always been known that the content of one's work is a motivating factor, contemporary organizations are required to create credible assignments where individuals can understand why they make an effort to perform. Unfortunately, organizations are designed by defining abstract tasks which are very far from being able to convey the value of the employee's contribution.

Liberty

The contradiction between the need to control what happens within an organization and the need to take advantage of human initiative and innovation is one of the paradoxes of organizational design. In fact, while we can envision an organization that works as a perfect machine, we know that the contingencies that any organization has to face in its relationship with the market make it impossible for this machine to really be perfect and performing at the same time. Therefore, while we know that in more stable and standardized processes substituting human discretion with automation has a great impact, we are forced to recognize that no organization is so stable that it can undertake such substitution at all levels and in all its processes. The increase in volatility, uncertainty, complexity, and ambiguity (the so-called VUCA world) requires organizations to increase their capacity to adapt, and this can be fulfilled only by granting more discretion to employees.

Inglehart (2015) describes the pressure for more liberty as a consequence of societal values that concentrate more on the individual's well-being, autonomy and self-expression. Organizational design has too long been conceived as a way to normalize behaviors and ensure that the organization responds in standardized, accountable, and replicable ways. As such, organizations have not allowed individuals to express themselves fully. Many energies are constrained into activities, which are related to one's objectives (for example, performing to be promoted), but might not be in tune with the goals of the organization. An example is what Orpen (1994) found when he described how career outcomes might be dependent on other factors than real contribution to performance, or even individual performance. The evolution of societal values exposes existing organizations to many threats. It can be considered one of the reasons why many talented employees flee from established organizations to work at start-ups or become entrepreneurs.

Cooperation

Chester Barnard (1938) first proposed considering organizations as evolved forms of cooperation among individuals. He argued that they could be seen as traces of the evolutionary path of the human species, given its extraordinary ability to perform complex tasks. Cooperation has always been at the core of organizational design in its endeavor to integrate tasks that had been distributed across roles and units. According to Lawrence and Lorsch (1967), once the design has differentiated among organizational units, the designer should then invest in integration to ensure that the different parts stick together and perform as a single body. More recently, the issue of cooperation has been part of the discussion on emerging forms of network organization where different parts or legal entities or even separate organizations cooperate to produce systemic performances (Baker et al., 1992). Despite its presence in several theories on organizational design, cooperation is not considered the basic force, the inner driver, of organizational life when it comes to human resources and employees. Rather, organizations have emphasized competition, as testified by the spread of the idea of talent-based competition in the design of human resource management models

(Cappelli, 2008). The emerging values in society point in a different direction, one where organizations let people gather around challenges where they actively cooperate to solve problems and innovate. The need to belong, which is present in the analysis by Inglehart, is expressed in the need for an organizational environment where people seek to cooperate and perceive themselves as part of a collective effort.

Sense

All the changes that we have re-connected across different streams of research like societal change, SDT, and phenomenology have one foundation: the search for meaning and sense in one's actions. Our societies are abandoning the time when people would accept a role and act accordingly to define paths to self-realization through the many opportunities being offered. The rebirth of the individual celebrated in this book starts from here, from the recognition that each individual is endowed with many more qualities and abilities than those required by structured tasks, and can and should find ways to realize his/her own potential. While role systems and attributed tasks have been central components of traditional organizational design, the changes that are occurring urge organizations to rebuild themselves on sense: that is, making explicit the merit, the reason, and the desirability of what the organization produces.

In conclusion, societal change and individual, universal basic needs point in the same direction, and they pressure organizations to adopt a different approach to design (Table 2.2), which is urgently needed to survive the coming paradigm shift.

Organizations that fail to rethink their structure and processes in this direction will face increasing levels of disengagement. While this is very evident in Western countries, it is rapidly spreading to other countries as well. Work conditions and work/life balance are being reclaimed by employees all over the globe, and it is illusionary to think that the coming changes can be limited to organizations in richer countries. What makes these processes unique is that, instead of being animated by an ideological stance, as happened with mass unionization, they are rooted in the desire of each individual to be perceived as unique and valuable, and not to be considered as simply part of a class or a group.

Table 2.2 A consistent stream of changes

SDT (Ryan and Deci)	Societal change (Inglehart)	Organizational design principles
Autonomy	Self-realization	Liberty
Competence	Esteem	Sense
Relatedness	Belonging	Cooperation

2.3 A new alliance between society and the individual

The past few years in social sciences, and in management as one of them, have been dominated by two opposing trends. On the one side, there is mainstream research, which is highly empiricist, which means that it derives implications from empirical research often "in the past tense" (to identify the fact that it can look only at processes that have already happened), despite the fact that it is organized into very different paradigms, schools, and approaches. On the other side, there is the combative group of critical, radical, Marxian researchers who oppose mainstream views by considering structures of domination, control, and exploitation, and accusing mainstream research of being "the left of the right," as Bourdieu would put it.

Besides, there is an abundance of practitioner-oriented books, articles, and papers which do not even consider the problems of methodology and the limits of easy generalizations from a handful of successful experiences (and we could doubt whether they might be really successful, given the selective bias).

It consequently comes as no surprise that there is no serious debate on the structure of knowledge best suited to understanding how organizations will evolve. Researchers and practitioners alike are stuck in the (same) mud, which is a mixture of empiricism and historicism. They are both stuck because they only use past experiences to develop theories and implications, while it is clear that social sciences deal with phenomena which are affected by too many variables to be held constant in time and space. It does not make a great difference, therefore, if the methods are valid, as in peer-reviewed research, or not, as in most practitioner research. It is rather controversial if we compare this state of affairs with what has happened in sociology, where grand narratives of the world-to-be like those of Castells, Bauman, Beck, and Sennett have become mainstream and are animating the debate on the nature of contemporary societies in their evolution beyond post-modernism. Management books that take up the same challenge are usually not rigorous, and mainstream scholars avoid the challenge. As a consequence, we can only access accounts of the future of organizations which are not based on rigorous analysis and follow the fashion of the moment.

Unfortunately, when it comes to management theory and academic research there is an evident lack of a debate along the same lines of thought as those which animate sociology, considering the respective role of individuals and systems as protagonists of the coming changes. In fact, a major consequence of this neglect has been the demise of the individual actor as a protagonist of social action. Several social scientists have attempted to define a way to reconcile actors and systems (Berger and Luckmann, 1967), and there are models which account for the interdependence between the two. For example, most social scientists are familiar with the structuration approach of Giddens (1986), according to which, actors create novel structures of interaction in the interplay between their free will and interests and the already-existing social structures. In turn, the novel structures of interaction can be solidified into social structures which are then propagated and established to become taken for granted.

However, most research in management either disregards the issue or simply assumes structure as the most relevant factor. When considered explicitly, individuals are seen as isolated individuals (for example, entrepreneurs) who have had a specific impact, rather than research being based on assumptions and deductions concerning an explicit praxeology of individuals and their actions. Individual actors are either heroes or do not exist, which is the consequence of a neglect of the real complexity of organizational action. Contrary to this naïve description, those who work in and with organizations cannot but appreciate the interplay between structure and action. I personally have worked with numerous organizations and encountered many individuals who shared with me accounts of their efforts to act. Most of these descriptions were very clear as to how the structured, institutionalized nature of organizations had played a major role in impeding any relevant action or change. At the same time, their accounts highlighted the heroism required to confront organizations in order to make a change. While I acknowledge that I met some individuals who were hiding behind the limits and constraints of structured organizations, most of them were not. My research into organizational change slowly drove me away from the idea of individual and organizational resistance to recognition of how much of the challenge instead arises from the fact that organizations are systems designed not to change.

I once had the chance to support the global HR team of a company headquartered in Geneva, Switzerland. The company was global but had originated from a merger of two companies. Its global structure was highly decentralized, and every country had been able to design its own HR processes. The project that I was asked to advise had the goal of defining a unified competency framework at the global level as part of an effort to centralize competence management. The team was composed of representatives of the major countries and/or regions. While the team worked very collaboratively in defining the needs, individuals were conditioned by their local HR departments to make sure that the new system would be easy to align with the existing one. Since there were more than ten different competency models, the task was very difficult. I could experience all the frustration of managers in the team over the impossibility of getting rid of old systems to promote innovation. The constraints were all organizational, such as the need to change the HRIS or the need to change forms and procedures.

More recently, I have come across an important Italian luxury goods company which issued a request for proposals for a new competency model in a very ambitious document which detailed the need to be innovative. Upon further inquiry, however, the HR function revealed that they wanted a simple restyling. As I pressed them to explain the apparent non-alignment between the document and their explicit needs, they revealed that while on paper they thought the system was outdated and needed a complete rethinking, that would have had too many consequences in terms of changing processes, procedures, forms, and so on. Therefore they were left with the sub-optimal choice of a quick fix, which would not really make it more effective.

I have numerous similar examples, and any of my readers probably can come up with many more. They all point to the fact that whilst we simplistically attribute resistance to people, its true sources are to be found in organizational structures and processes themselves.

However, I sense that there is hope. The time has come for actors to reclaim their central place in organizations. The description of universal basic needs and emerging societal values in the two previous sections testifies to the resurgence of the individual in the molding of society, and it provides the conditions for the emergence of a different paradigm for organized activity, which should be based on individual liberty and freedom to choose. This may sound controversial if we consider the current turmoil in different areas of the world, with the resurgence of ideological fundamentalism. As I stated above, I personally consider this turmoil to be a reaction to the emergence of ambiguity between a traditional society, based on institutions framed by command and control principles, and the spread of the idea that individuals are the protagonists of society. It clearly assumes different forms in different societies. In more structured societies, the ambiguity is so great that some individuals find it difficult to come to terms with freedom to choose and resort to extremism as a form of renewed certainty. In less structured societies, the same ambiguity creates pressures toward the demise of existing institutions; but in the absence of a different model for societal collaboration, this drive towards less institutionalization risks being perceived as nihilist. The intensity of these forces is directly proportional to how close we are to a different model of social organization.

As has happened in the past century, business organizations in their constant struggle to outcompete others have been at the forefront of experimentation. The magnificent force of evolution has urged them to continue experimenting. As Schumpeter (2013) so clearly explained, our business environment is constantly the arena for a process of creative destruction by virtue of which new organizations, products, and services replace older ones. While this process tends to be associated with strategy in terms of products and services offered, it has an analogy in the competition among different organizational forms, i.e. ways of organizing work within organizations. In fact, if we consider popular descriptions of the best companies to work for, and the list of the most recognized organizations in management, we find that many of them are moving toward the adoption of structures, processes, and values which radically depart from those that have been common in the past. This is of particular importance in areas where organizations operate in close proximity to each other, so that they end up struggling to attract the best human capital possible. This is the story of places like Silicon Valley, but also of major urban areas like Greater London in the UK or Milan in Italy. When a resource becomes scarce, entrepreneurs are urged to think of ways to gain access to it by outcompeting others.

I am not fond of the common eulogy to private business organizations, and I recognize that they have important limitations which this book attempts to address by guiding towards novel ways of organizing. However, I feel a glimmer of hope. Social change and the diffusion of the value of the individual, each single individual, are bringing about a scenario which may depart from the world of annihilation based on objectification that has been so well described by Foucault (1995).

While Foucault linked modernity with the demise of the individual in flesh and blood substituted by an object measured by powerful institutions like the education system or business organizations, I sense that this stage of human history is coming to an end, and that it is giving way to an individual-centered society. The emergent views in social sciences that I have described, like SDT and Inglehart's theory, bear witness to a resurgence of the individual. While society has compressed our individuality through powerful collective ideologies, as Simmel (1972) realized, individuals can never be reduced to their social sphere. Modernity attempted to annihilate individuality, as well described by Foucault, but we can protect it until the time comes when individuality is once again at the center of society.

3 Organizations: the enemy within

In the previous chapter I described the powerful pressures that are revitalizing the role of the individual within contemporary society. After the long period when individuals seemed to be dominated by systems reinforced by the power of organizational design, I foresee the emergence of a context where organizing assumes a completely different meaning. The power of systems designed on the basis of goals and ideologies has been well described by Foucault (1995) in his critique of the objectification of human beings in modernity, as well as by Burawoy (1982), who spent time as a blue-collar worker in both Western and Communist factories. Burawoy provided ample evidence that the texture of how work had been organized impacted on the level of oppression of workers. Despite the existence of two very different political, economic, and social systems, organizing replicated the same compression of individual identity. However, the time has now come to hope for a different approach to organizing corporations, and possibly social systems. The pressures for change that I have analyzed stem from two processes: one at the individual level, with the urge to satisfy the three universal basic needs of autonomy, competence and relatedness; and one at the societal level, with the emergence of post-materialism (Inglehart, 2015), and the demand by individuals to live fuller lives.

One frequently listens to debates on the balance between personal life and work where the speakers express a clear bias towards the idea that business needs come first, and that people must find decent ways to lead their lives in the interstices of their work. I personally think that this trade-off is a consequence of how we have separated work from our lives so that it is a necessary component of our membership of societies but not a cornerstone of our life projects. At the same time, those speakers reveal that we are biased by the profound belief that technical systems come first, and that their optimization should be guaranteed before individuals are taken into account. But the changes taking place around us point in a different direction, one characterized by the centrality of human action, innovativeness, and engagement.

The disbelief with which this simple statement will be met is a symptom of how rooted the traditional view of organizations has become. As commonly happens with radical changes, the world that we live in has been shaped by values and principles that are radically different from those now emerging. Our institutions in the broader sense have inherited the values of the twentieth century, which largely contributed to their formation. The concepts of state, public administration, and business organization have all been coined during the modern era and are clearly indebted to a specific value system which is now disappearing. As Stinchcombe (1965) pointed out, they are shaped on a social technology which is outdated. Their guiding principles reflect the power of formalization in terms of writing, and their structural characteristics are molded according to the idea that the best decisions require a hierarchy of command and control to be taken and subsequently enacted.

I am not surprised, therefore, when I meet managers, even brilliant ones, who cannot even conceive of a world that might not be in charge of organizations through power and control. However, I try to explain what is really happening around those managers, and help them question the assumption that they are changing the world or even their organization. Of course, they have an important impact on the internal and external environment when they promote strategic changes or reorganizations. They affect a large number of individuals when they launch a new product or downsize their workforce. However, the reality of their everyday work is highly symbolic in nature. They do not do anything practically, they manipulate symbols and ideas. While its intent is satirical, the description of a top manager's life by Stanley Bing in his monthly column in the magazine *Fortune*, probably conveys a more realistic picture than we think. Top managers (and most managers) are engaged in symbolic battles over what is happening around them. They receive help in interpreting numbers, devising stories which account for the numbers that they observe and those that they promise to other stakeholders. They talk to each other, attempting to make things happen. Occasionally they take decisions and expect them to be implemented in the organization. I do not want to give the impression that I consider this not useful, or that it is easy or trivial. I think that it is an incredible accomplishment which rests on the ability for powerful storytelling which can be converted into story-doing by making others engaged and supportive. However, it does not rest on their hierarchical power alone. While power may play a role, the ability to promote real action does not require it to have consequences, and on the contrary it is often affected by the limitations of individual decision makers which have been clearly described by research on decision making and are at the roots of why liberals do not believe in centralized decision-making systems.

Given the disbelief of those in charge of contemporary organizations when confronted with the challenges I have described, those who are in charge of the ultimate storytelling on what is appropriate to do in business, the resistance to change of organizations will be one of the factors that more successfully oppose change pressures. After all, modern organizations have been shaped to guarantee that they operate in reliable and accountable ways, and in order to do so they are packed with mechanisms that control standardization and reduce variability. Organizations hire candidates who very closely follow an ideal model, many times disregarding the consequences. Some time ago I had a conversation with the CEO of one of the largest consulting firms in Italy. We were talking about the need to adopt a more evidence-based approach to hiring and recruitment. He confessed his dissatisfaction with the high level of voluntary turnover that his company had been experiencing, and moved on to consider that, given its reputation, it hired only the top graduates from the best colleges in Milan and Rome. What if this ideal model was not working? What if the company could obtain much better results with a different goal, maybe enriching the diversity of people that it hired? I was impressed by how clear he was on this, and yet nothing had changed. So I asked him why. "I can't prove that I'm right, so we resolve to going on with the old approach," was his answer. The organizational system, once again, had taken over, and not even the CEO could reverse it.

How organizations have evolved has made them a full-fledged ideal type or stable configuration which is designed in a way that minimal changes to its pure form will yield negative results. This is a self-reinforcing mechanism which is one of the powerful sources of inertia. As I mentioned in the previous chapter, we too often interpret inertia as resistance by individuals, while it is probably rooted in the interconnectedness of the different elements that make up organizations. They have co-evolved with the goal of making organizations ever more predictable under the competitive and evolutionary pressure of markets and competition. Contemporary organizations have been marvelous in guaranteeing the accountability and reliability that we experience today. In doing so, however, they have made change from within increasingly difficult, to the point that when they are required to react flexibly to changes they tend to fail rather than change (Carroll and Hannan, 2000).

The resistance to change embedded in organizations is consistent with the description by Roberts (2007) of complementarities in organizational forms. According to Roberts, complementarities among different organizational characteristics reinforce a pure model, making it a stable configuration. The different components can be either the product of a rational design effort or the consequence of evolutionary processes (I clearly favor the latter over the former, which is instead assumed by Roberts), but what is relevant is that the consequences remain the same: attempting to change some of these characteristics will not produce advantages until changes are so massive that the organization moves from one configuration to another. This may explain how change processes in organizations are often derailed by the absence of clear performance advantages in the early stages.

I have often encountered organizations which had retreated from ambitious change projects because of a lack of results in the earlier stages. I have recently supported a large organization which had the goal of promoting diversity and inclusion at the global level. This large, global company had launched an ambitious project to measure the organizational diversity climate, and the HR department had collected ideas and suggestions from employees all over the world. Top managers were very determined and allocated many resources to the project. However, after a very rigorous analysis, when they launched the first actions, they could not provide evidence of the results and the impact on performance, having to retreat very rapidly in the face of criticism from managers less concerned with diversity than with business. My comment to them was that when you attempt such a profound change, you cannot overhaul the organization unless you have been given enough time. At first, as Roberts has also pointed out, you can even worsen your results.

According to the idea of complementarity, it should be expected that the changes that I have discussed above will find it difficult to transform existing organizations, and that a radical shift will be needed to create the organization of the future. Interestingly, the handful of examples of organizations which have already adopted some radically different features consists of start-ups or new organizations, while established ones are lagging behind in their change efforts. This very basic fact further induces me to think that the changes are necessary, but so profound that the change effort will need to be proportionate. That means that courage is needed to sustain this change even through a long transition phase.

In this perspective, I think that the managers and leaders of our institutions (public and private) should recognize that their first enemy is their own organization, and the principles according to which it has been designed and managed in the past. In a sense the enemy is within. I shall try to explain why.

3.1 Organizations compress freedom

The emergence of modern organizations marked a great leap forward in the ability to produce goods and services. The advantage of economies of scale spread throughout the economy thanks to the ability of the new giants to coordinate a myriad of transactions that would make it impossible to work in a simple market economy. In its turn, this change exerted pressure for increasing standardization at all levels. Tools, procedures, instruments, and component parts would increasingly become the same, allowing organizations to spread production among different suppliers.

The emergence of the new organizations has been so accurately described by Alfred Chandler (1977) that it would be of no practical use to summarize it here. However, it is important to realize that the impressive changes in the economy of the twentieth century originated from the emergence of a new model of organization which responded adequately to the challenges that our predecessors faced.

The new organization was heavily based on the role of management, as a chain of transmission between the operations and the apex of the organization. Managers were in charge of assuring continuity in business operations, and directing the efforts and attention of workers at the various levels. They grew to become the major infrastructure of these emerging giants. It was by virtue of this structure that amazing projects were launched and completed. One can think of the construction of the railways connecting the east and west coasts of the USA or Canada as marvelous examples of organizations on an incredible scale. Thereafter, the same approach was extended to factories, which started producing at an unprecedented pace.

In strict analogy with the biological world, larger organizations became immense beehives where everybody knew their role and acted accordingly. The deal was to give up one's autonomy and initiative to follow rules, procedures, and approaches dictated by a rational analysis of what would be more effective and productive. This was the dawn of the reign of a scientific and rational approach to managing organization and work. The ideas of Frederick Winslow Taylor enjoyed global reach and laid the foundations for a new way of organizing which successfully completed the paradigm transition that Taylor had anticipated as necessary.

Whilst in the past century the model needed remodeling, its basic framework is still unchanged. In fact, its resilience is such that changes can be made at its periphery, but its roots are extremely stable. The need to respond to a heterogeneous market promoted the emergence of the M-form shaped according to the intuition of Alfred Sloan at General Motors in the 1930s. The perception that different customers might be better served by different brands and models of cars led Sloan to hypothesize that his organization in turn would need to specialize activities at the level of brands. GM transformed from an integrated automobile producer into a conglomerate composed of diverse divisions, each managed separately and competing in a different segment of the market. The role of boundary spanning units like marketing and other staff grew substantially in the 1950s. Whilst the core of the company had long been its manufacturing unit, the recognition of fluctuations between production and consumption, as well as understanding of the financial costs associated with inventory, led to the creation of units whose purposes were to stabilize production and selling fluxes.

Internationalization and the emergence of multinational organizations promoted the creation of corporate and hub-and-spokes models across the world in the 1960s and 1970s. Operating in foreign countries posed many challenges to organizations. Local regulations were different, customers had different habits and tastes, employees expected different treatment. At the same time, operating as a global company meant that some processes and procedures had to be aligned. The importance of quality and reduction of slack resources forced a refocus on the operational side in the 1980s as Japanese car makers taught the world a different path to large-scale manufacturing. The failure to predict patterns in the market put the emphasis more on reactivity than planning. The new factory had to be "lean," which meant it had to operate with the least inventory possible, which could be obtained by devolving part of decision making to operational units. In the 1990s, the obsession with operating effectiveness extended to the large staff units and gave rise to changes intended to make organizations leaner. Downsizing targeted the excess workforce which had populated the head-quarters. Management layers were reduced and in general, personnel costs came under close scrutiny. New information technology coupled with the creation of an extensive transportation network spanning the globe led to the decoupling of large organizations into networks of separate legal entities in the 2000s. Outsourcing and offshoring became tools to reduce operating costs further and to achieve more flexibility. And it is not over yet. Today, organizations are trying as hard as they can to incorporate principles deriving from the diffusion of loosely coupled but active structures like social networks based on social media and digital collaboration technologies.

If we consider its persistence after more than a century, we cannot but recognize that this model has proved to be highly adaptive; hence one would be tempted to consider it able to face the coming changes. Formal organizations have established themselves and evolved in terms of different forms and areas. They have become a very successful element of modernity. Whenever a new problem arises or there is an opportunity to be taken, a new organization is defined to deal with it. From the evolutionary point of view, formal organizations are winners. Other forms of social action have been dismantled or marginalized. Cooperative forms, for example, have assumed characteristics that are ever more similar to those of traditional business organizational forms. Spontaneous social movements increasingly establish formal organizational forms to support their agendas. Even counter-system movements have transformed themselves into formal organizations.

An example from the city where I live most of the time, Milan in Italy, is the Centro Sociale Leoncavallo. It was created in 1975 as a space for social and political aggregation for counter-movements generally inspired by criticism of capitalism. It all started from the occupation of a private building in Via Leoncavallo. The Centro Sociale went through many changes over 40 years, but it gave rise to many different activities and sources for self-financing. Today it is an impressive reality in the cultural landscape of Milan, and the building which hosts it is rented to the Centro at the price of €500 000 per year, an astounding amount for something which started out as a fringe movement in the difficult and violent 1970s. The Centro is today a highly complex organization, which despite ideological prudery is run as a formal organization with some more levels of democracy but as well managed as a business organization, offering courses, concerts, a hemp bar, a coffee shop, etc.

Hence formal organizations reign all around us, even in places where they would be largely unexpected, like extreme left-wing social movements. Despite the success, however, I think that at times of change, the past is no judge of what will happen tomorrow. It is precisely for this reason that top managers are risking so much if they disregard the many signs of coming change described in the first two chapters of this book. Given their experience, top managers cannot be blamed for trusting their organizational model, but the nature of being a manager should be the ability to think differently. In fact, given that we cannot find evidence of a structural intellectual superiority of managers, I think we should expect them at least to be able to frame situations and contexts differently. This is the essence of storytelling, which is a way to reframe reality and infuse it with new sensemaking.

This book is a manifesto intended to make everybody realize that change is occurring all around us, despite the fact that we do not realize its full potential. The reason why managers should realize this is the fact that some basic tenets of what is required, available, and acceptable in organizations are going to change. I discussed this process at great length in the previous chapter. I shall now try to explain why so many organizations seem to be ignoring it because they are structurally unable to face what it requires them to change.

The basic element of organizational design is the belief that we can anticipate what will occur and program our organization to choose the best possible alternative course of action. Structuration is precisely this, the predisposition of tools, procedures, and behaviors in advance so that when an event occurs, the organization is able to respond in a semi-automatic or automatic way, each time following the very same pattern of actions (reliability). This is nothing new. It is one way to explain organizations that is connected to Herbert Simon's view of them as decision-making collectives (Guetzkow and Simon, 1955). Simon conceptualized organizations as collective decision makers able to substitute pre-defined actions for recurrent decisions, thereby economizing in time. Let me explain this with a very simple example.

Whenever you enter the branch of a bank, you do so with the intent of performing several different actions that are of immediate interest to you as a customer. Clearly, you need first to identify the bank as the focal organization for your problem. So it is highly unrealistic to enter a bank to buy a loaf of bread, but much more realistic to do so because you need to inquire about a check that you have cashed. As you enter the bank, you will direct your attention to the area, office, and/or person in the bank branch that you presume might provide an answer. Hopefully, the organization has designed its layout to facilitate your search with signals, visual clues, or maybe a greeter to help you choose where to go. Several banks have installed devices to assist you in identifying your turn and the expected waiting time, like monitors with your name or a number assigned to you upon entering the branch. Once you establish contact with the focal person, s/he will follow a set of procedures and rules to respond to your request by choosing among a limited set of alternatives. At some banks, s/he will be free to decide how to greet you; at others s/he may be required to follow a service script.

The design of the branch down to the tools and even the relational approach of the employees will be made so that the service encounters are as effective and efficient as possible. Instead of facing several decisions as separate problems to deal with, the design allows all actors (customers and employees in this specific case) to choose pre-defined options and follow them through.

In a simple world, this works well. Now let us make it more complex. First, you might imagine that the customer has a more complex problem, one that requires advice from an expert, maybe a financial issue with some tax consequences to sort out. Still, this can be dealt with by specializing roles, and defining a separate space/area where the customer can engage in lengthier conversations with the expert. Let us add more complexity. The bank may decide to compete on a set of services which extend from purely financial ones to other domains, for example because it feels the pressure of online providers of services like Amazon. This in turn adds complexity to the kind of requests that the customer may come up with, and makes structured design harder. But it is not only an issue on the side of the customer. The employees may grow increasingly dissatisfied by the limited autonomy and meaning of repeating the same structured encounters every day and reduce their level of engagement and commitment. They are no longer content with the simple fact of having a job and being paid but look for more enjoyment in their work. Things become even more complicated if we imagine that the customer is not entering a real branch but connecting by remote over the telephone, internet, or one day a virtual branch. The complexity increases rapidly as a product of all the variance that may be in place, and it can quite easily reach a level where pre-defined roles and tasks no longer suffice. My point is that this level has been reached in many different domains of our lives, at least in more economically advantaged countries. However, the way in which we design organizations is still a powerful means to compress alternatives at different levels, reducing our range of action at a time when we demand more freedom to act. Let us explore how this reduction of our freedom is occurring from the perspective of different stakeholders.

Customers

Organizations are adept at reducing our ability to find exactly what we want. While modernization has brought an incredible variety of products, it has limited the demand for variety from each single producer.

An example is what has happened to the way we dress ourselves. As a boy in the early 1970s I well remember that I would occasionally accompany my father and my mother to a man named Pancin in my home town of Trento. He had a one-window shop close to home, and he was a tailor. It is not that my family was rich; back then men and women would get their clothes tailor-made. My parents could choose the fabrics, then the style, and order minor adjustments that they considered more attractive. A garment was an act of specific creation. Ten years later, when I walked past the window of the shop I found it empty. Mister Pancin had given up in the wake of much cheaper (and more importantly, ready-to-use) clothes that could be easily bought at a fraction of the cost, and time. Today, we have gone even further because we can buy extraordinarily cheap clothes at shops like Zara and H&M in Europe or Ross and T.J. Maxx in the USA. And they come with a great deal of variety as well, given that they change by the day if not by the hour as new items are put on sale. Formal organizations offer much, but they require us to adapt to their sizes instead of their adapting to our sizes and desires.

Contemporary organizations provide us with a path to what they have decided to let us find. In a sense they do not decide for us; rather, they define the alternatives among which we are allowed to make our choice. While this made sense when people's expectations for heterogeneity were low and they would be happy just to find a few alternatives to fulfill their needs, in today's terms this is a major limitation. In fact, personalization is striking back, and we witness the resurgence of tailors and tailor-made products and services. The problem is not that formal organizations are unwilling to respond to our needs; rather, they are built in a way that makes it very problematic and expensive to do so. Any increase in the complexity that they have to deal with is a menace to their ability to define in advance what to do, who does what, and who controls the results. It is by virtue of this reduction of the possible alternatives that they can prove themselves highly effective and efficient. In some sense, the price of their efficiency has been the reduction of the effectiveness that we can take advantage of. This trade-off is tempered by the fact that the extraordinary growth of markets has allowed many players to compete with each other, replacing the possibility of personalization at a single shop with the choice of many alternatives at different shops. However, even this comes at a cost for us. In fact, it reduces our ability to find the right product or services, thus increasing the search costs. True, the internet gives us a helping hand by enabling us to compare the offers of different competitors on dedicated websites. Yet the alternatives are fixed, and we are bound to choose among them or go for the resurgent tailor-made alternative.

In sum, formal organizations have benefited us by reducing costs and diffusing products and services. It is clear that this reduction of alternatives has some advantages. But while it allows for a compression of the costs associated with most products and services, it does so at the expense of our desire to be unique and find the perfect match between our desires and what we buy and/or use. Whether this compression of our alternatives (and ultimately our freedom as consumers) will still be justified in the future depends on the hidden reduction of value that it imposes on us. Good news may be on the way, however. Firstly, these costs are associated with a traditional idea of how we produce products and deliver services, which may not be the same as the one emerging with the diffusion of 3D printers and ubiquitous digital technologies. Moreover, we have well understood that when a producer is able to increase its capacity to personalize its products/services while controlling the relative costs, it enjoys a great market advantage.

The issue may be less straightforward than I have described it if we consider that also deciding what we really want is costly in terms of cognitive effort and time. Hence it might well be that the correct solution lies in a conscious and balanced search for a more fine-grained set of alternatives to choose from, as in the idea of the "nudge" popularized by Thaler and Sunstein (2009). However, it is clear that as consumers we have been constrained by the emergence of formal organizations so obsessed with standardization.

Employees

The compression of freedom that has resulted from formal organizations is even more evident in the case of employees. The way in which organizations are designed assigns individuals to roles defined by sets of tasks. The process by which design occurs moves from the identification of goals to the analysis of technical constraints which defines the bases for identification of the tasks to be assigned to roles, and subsequently the individuals who will assume those same roles. It is true that, over time, the description of tasks has become somewhat blurred, but the idea that human resources are framed alongside roles is still strongly held by most managers. In fact, contemporary micro design assigns an important role to defining a few general tasks, and (apparently) allowing individuals to define how to perform those tasks. In reality, the technological determination of many processes and the interconnectedness of organizations (and roles) impose so many constraints on individual freedom that it appears to be mostly on paper. The degrees of freedom of individuals within existing formal organizations are in reality much narrower than formally stated. In fact, even managers are constrained by so many procedures, roles, habits, and expectations that it is common to hear them complain of the difficulty of making any major changes to their organizations. Despite the fact that there have been few attempts to liberate the energy of individuals, for example through empowering them or increasing autonomy and discretion locally, the value of initiative and innovativeness in established organizations is questionable. Once again in the press and in public keynote speeches, top managers and management gurus declare the need to liberate the energy of individuals within organizations, but the test of reality points in a radically different direction. An interesting example has been popularized by the media in their account of how a Kodak employee invented a prototype of the digital camera but was not supported by top managers at the company, who did not believe in the technology, feared its consequences for their business models (and their careers?), and preferred to act in a conservative way (Estrin, 2015). Although this brief example might be easily attributed to the shortsightedness of managers, a closer look reveals that it was more a consequence of the many constraints imposed by organizations. Some of these constraints are highly visible and formally stated (consider explicit procedures); others are built into the everyday work of the organization as routines, habits, stratified expectations, and so forth.

Despite all the cheap talk on the importance of human capital, most organizations act in a way that each employee can be seen as easily substitutable. Relying on formal tasks and jobs gives the (false) impression that it is the design that governs what happens within an organization. We know that this is a partial truth, since human behavior can be influenced, but not completely constrained even by the most inhumane organization or a total institution like a prison. As a consequence of this state of affairs, however, employees are subject to human resources practices which are framed by tasks and job descriptions. Human resources practices are driven by the desire to attract and retain employees who fit the model, rather than truly innovative and visionary contributors. As I always point out to my HR friends, they are the watchdogs of conformity within organizations. They define who will be admitted, and who will succeed on the basis of an undisputed, *ex-ante*, but entirely non-evidence-based approach that links tasks to human-level characteristics. While much of the energy goes into defining more refined tools to measure fit, I argue that the perspective is wrong from its premises. Even if we were able completely to judge the best fit of humans to tasks, we would not contribute to long-term performance (and maybe even have issues with short-term performance).

Managers and top executives

The ways in which organizations frame their relationships with employees are inspired by an idea of command and control. While no executive would explicitly accept the view of organizations projected by Fritz Lang's movie *Metropolis*, most of them fear the loss of control caused by a revision of this model. In fact, it is commonplace to hear executives question the opportuneness of opening internal social networks where employees are allowed to share their opinions with no control or surveillance. Limiting the freedom of employees, however, has important consequences for managers as well, because it restricts their ability to fulfill a more complete role.

While on paper executives should be in charge of managing the organization and promoting change and innovation, their daily routines are mostly characterized by conservation of the *status quo*. A great deal of effort is spent on making sure that the organization continues to operate smoothly by replicating what was successful in the past, or even worse what has been designed, irrespective of whether it is effective. I have heard several managers complain of the complexity of a competence model or a performance management form, but then continue to use it. Managers enjoy the advantage of a job higher up the hierarchical scale which entitles them to progressively higher salaries, but the true autonomy that they can have is severely limited.

Whilst in good times this can be rather pleasant, it becomes a real burden when the organization is going through hard times. On the basis of their position, managers are expected to have the levers to reverse a bad performance, while in practical terms they tend to be hostages to the existing organization, with little opportunity to demonstrate their abilities to change. And if they were given that opportunity, the interconnectedness of organizations makes initiative and boldness characteristics which are hardly ever rewarded. It is more advisable to promote changes that have been legitimated by reputed consultants than to envision a future for the business. It does not come as a surprise that the most inspiring leaders are not managers and/or executives but entrepreneurs who have created their organizations as acts of self-fulfillment, and not as instruments for the rationalization of routine actions.

Investors

It may seem odd, but even investors are constrained by the way in which we organize. In fact, the obsession with control pushes organizations to restrain their innovativeness and initiative to promote incremental changes, which at times are only limited fixes, which do not hold in time. In doing so, they limit the possibility of investors to be rewarded, while at the same time severely diminishing the viability of the organization in the long run.

While investors may move from one organization to another on the basis of the more or less positive economic outlook, they have no guarantees that their resources are being invested to yield the highest returns. The pressure to conform with the nature of the existing organization is such that resources are allocated more with a risk-averse bias than on the basis of prospective returns on investment. Formal organizations can safeguard investment through the complex pattern of connections that limit too much change, but by doing so they also constrain innovation, and the search for the so-called "blue oceans," those where profits can be reaped without engaging in fierce competition (Kim and Mauborgne, 2005).

In conclusion, the removal of risk and unpredictability within organizations does not remove them from the markets and from reality. Risk and unpredictability are the fundamental elements of competition, entrepreneurship, and markets. Without them, no economic value can be created and no competitive advantage can be maintained.

However, from the formal organization's perspective the removal of risk and unpredictability shields it for a limited time from the challenges of globalization and hyper-competition. Organizations tend to reinforce stability because they have been designed to do so, and they have been designed so well that they really enforce it, even when asked to innovate. I have discussed the advantages of this ability but, as clearly illustrated, the price to be paid is the constraint of autonomy and initiative which severely limits freedom for many different actors and prevents them from preparing the organization adequately for its future. Moreover, it creates a great deal of waste because of the need to destroy existing organizations to make room for new ones. While a certain degree of creative destruction is probably highly advisable, many organizations simply fail because they cannot escape from the self-imposed constraints of their formal organization. While at a more general level, the substitution of incumbent with novel organizations has worked well, a top manager would probably be concerned with this perspective. It is for this reason that top managers should rethink their role and prepare their organizations for change.

3.2 The illusion of leadership as an actor for change

A skeptic would counter my arguments by pointing to the many successful change processes that have taken place at large companies in the past few years. It is true that examples abound. Take IBM for example, which moved from a manufacturing company to a service giant, retaining its value while dismissing its computer and printer businesses. Or FCA, which merged two laggards like Fiat and Chrysler into a viable new company increasingly respected in the markets.

Most of these changes did not come about through revision of the assumptions on the organizational design model to put in place, but rather through acts of extraordinary leadership, either individual or collective. The story of FCA cannot be told without stressing the impact of Sergio Marchionne, who moved from a rather obscure company like SGS SA to one of the iconic Italian companies, Fiat. In similar vein, the story of IBM is not a story of individual leadership (despite the role of Lou Gerstner in the 1990s) but of a consistent effort by an entire top management team to renew the business model.

So the skeptic might wonder whether organizations only suffer from bad leadership instead of a crisis of their organizational design models. It is time to answer this doubt, which I do consider reasonable.

Although research on organizational ecology (which was my field through most of the 1990s) greatly downplays the impact of management action, I am not contending that leaders, and inspired leaders even more so, do not play a major role in revitalizing organizations. In fact, the previous two examples and many more clearly indicate that one way for traditional organizations to sustain themselves is to reduce the scope of their actions and simplify their internal structure, thereby reducing the complexity to face at least for a limited time span by virtue of the ability of good leaders to focus and prioritize. I know that this statement is surprising, but most successful individual-led changes are exciting stories of a reduction of complexity by virtue of which the organization becomes more clearly focused and operates more efficiently. This is not a completely novel way out of complexity; in fact, it is heavily indebted to Galbraith (1995) and his organizational design model. According to Galbraith, in the face of increasing complexity, organizations can either diminish the complexity that they have to consider (by reducing their scale of action, creating duplicate organizational units, accepting more redundancy in how they operate, or controlling the environment through lobbying and political action) or enhance their ability to cope (by improving information systems, knowledge management, and internal collaboration). Galbraith further describes how the second alternative may be stronger than the first, even though difficult to activate.

Consistently with Galbraith's model, the true challenge is to find a way to change without reducing the scope of action, considering that markets constantly promote novel products and services which may easily cut into many established companies' profits. FCA and IBM are successful at the moment, but what if somebody else becomes better than them in managing complexity? They will be outcompeted. This is already happening in many industries. Insurance companies are coming under the pressure of companies like Amazon or Google, which can leverage their enormous databases of customers and their ease of contact. Automakers cannot feel safe as Google self-guided cars develop, or when they hear that Apple is considering moving into the personal mobility industry. These are clear examples that even reducing the scope of action, the metaphor of the organization as composed by a central brain (top management and the headquarters) and a peripheral system (local units and individuals), which largely executes orders is no longer effective. Even more troublesome is that the initial success of these actions can fool organizations into thinking that it is the competence of their leaders which can solve the problems. This wrong belief may be based on facts which should be carefully reconsidered. It is not the ability of leaders *per se*, but the reduction of complexity in decision making that contributes to solving some issues. However, when challenges abound, a further reduction of complexity will not be accomplished only by resorting to brave and competent leaders.

This comes as no surprise for those familiar with Hayek. In fact, he discussed a very similar process when comparing market economies to central planning. It is therefore interesting to use his ideas and extend them to the interior of large organizations.

In Hayek's view, the complexity of problems to be solved while governing the exchanges and the allocation of resources within an economic system is too high to be solved through a central agency, no matter how sophisticated it may be (Petsoulas, 2013). For Hayek, criticism of central planning was a key element of a broader attack on the emergence of centralized economies both in socialist countries and across Europe (Hayek, 2005). In defending the merit of the market as a means to coordinate economic decisions better, he related it to the concept of spontaneous order. A spontaneous order occurs when a multitude of different, apparently uncoordinated, processes result in an ordered outcome (Sugden, 1989). Markets generate spontaneous ordering on the basis of unrelated decisions by different and dispersed actors, without requiring any constructive interventions by external actors and/or institutions. In Hayek's view, markets emerged as evolutionary mechanisms that took root because of their effectiveness in coordinating decisions. In order for a planning system to obtain the same level of allocation, Hayek argued, we should postulate not only perfect rationality but also the availability of local information on any single actor involved, which would clearly be impossible to obtain.

Let us apply this line of thought to organizations. Most of them have grown so big that they are more similar in size to a local market than to an organization. At any time, a multitude of actors are taking decisions, allocating resources (for example their time and attention) to different problems, and exchanging information. Despite the illusion of control, all these processes are impossible to track. For this reason, organizations limit the alternatives through an organized system of rules, procedures, processes, and controls. In doing so, however, they act as planned economies, sacrificing the ability to be more effective and adaptable.

The alternative is to conceive organizations as aggregates of actors who generate a spontaneous order which can extend also beyond the formal boundaries of the organization. If you are familiar with the idea of open source innovation or crowdsourcing, you cannot but see the striking resemblance of these common processes in fostering innovation nowadays with the idea of spontaneous ordering. Guiding all these processes through a central authority is impossible, unless the organization decides to self-limit its capacity to innovate, be flexible, and adapt. Therefore, the recourse to leadership and strong or illuminated leaders will be of no help in the future.

3.3 We need to rethink how we organize to free individuals

Once we recognize that leadership is not the means to change organizations so that they can take up the challenges which lie ahead, we are left with the question of what should be done. The answer lies in the recognition that organizations are effective in relation to their ability to constrain individual behavior and action. The more they are able to do so, the better they operate, under conditions of an almost perfect match between what needs to be done and what organizations are designed to be doing. The true problem is here. In fact, increasing complexity makes it ever more unlikely that the match between what needs to be done and what has been designed will be obtained. So what is the way out of this dilemma?

The key factor is reversing the assumption that the best way to act collectively is to divide tasks among individuals and assign the role of governance to the organizational pyramid up to top management. Actually, even in today's organizations, research on organizational development and change has demonstrated that there is a lot more to this than meets the eye. In fact, while the formal organization is strictly designed to predetermine and control tasks and behaviors, the everyday life of an organization is punctuated by acts of discretion, and local, limited changes, which at times diffuse through the entire body of the organization. What I propose is not only to recognize this as a fact and to decouple it from the formal organization by labeling it the "informal" part of the organization, but also to recognize it as a basis for the design of the organization so as to leverage the potential of this multi-level distributed capacity to learn, adapt, and innovate.

It is my opinion that, although I limit my analysis to business organizations, some of the same trends are ongoing also within society and will soon affect the institutions that we use to coordinate our complex societal body.

In conclusion to this chapter, I want to point out the three (here again the power of three!) key requirements that ensue from the first three chapters and whose further development by virtue of the spread of pervasive communication and knowledge exchange will be dealt with in Chapter 4; this in turn will lead to a proposal for a different design of organizations in Chapter 5.

1. The first requirement is *to center organizations on the individual employee* (the human factor) *as opposed to the job or task.* The multifaceted nature of society entails that organizations must be able to understand the individual needs of their customers and personalize how they operate. The ability to maintain the advantage of standardization through technologies while allowing potentially unlimited personalization calls for an organizational system whereby adaptive decisions are being constantly taken by different actors. Some of those decisions will rely on the customer him/herself, as happens when people are allowed to personalize the look and feel of software; others will require that employees (or more broadly defined, members of the organization) are involved, as happens when customers request a variation on a beverage at their favorite coffee shop. In this manner, the concepts of job and designed task lose all significance. At most, they can still be analyzed and defined as very special circumstances to provide very general guidance for employees. There is no such thing as a task that can be described once and forever. Organizations need powerful and continuous systems of communication that convey the direction in which the system is moving with respect to the actions to be taken by the specific employee on the basis of his/her own local judgment. Abandoning the regime of the job description will have systemic consequences on labor markets, professions, human resource management practices, and in general on how individuals relate to organizations. A partial move in this direction is recognition that jobs in organizations result from complex patterns of job crafting by virtue of which individuals fit and tailor-make their work to their characteristics (Berg et al., 2008).

2. The second requirement is to *conceive organizations as complex, overlapping, adaptive relationships patterns* which are not constrained within their legal boundaries and operate as evolutionary systems in search of spontaneous ordering. It is evident that the transition to new organizational forms

will have profound impacts on incumbent organizations, with few of them being really able to transform so radically. Many will be replaced by emerging organizations because of the inertia and resistance to change described in long-term studies on organizational populations (Carroll and Hannan, 2000). Formal organizations are so obsessed with control and replication that most research on innovation can be re-interpreted as a search for ways to shield change against the normalizing effect of traditional organizational routines. In fact, organizations are frequently asked to create separate teams to promote innovation, or to create different policies to manage them. I find this very revealing of what constitutes the enemy to change and adaptability; it is an enemy within, so intertwined with everyday activity that it cannot be seen.

3. The third requirement is to *rethink the role of management in the direction of a corporate sensemaker* which learns from the emergent structures and experiments with the creation of links and connections across different domains of the organization. It should be clear here why I used a quote from Frederick Winslow Taylor in the first chapter of this book. It is a well-deserved homage to a world of organizations which is approaching its dusk. At the same time, I recognize that this will recreate a context where management should act more as a researcher than as an executor, as Taylor thought. I believe that in some sense we will witness the end of a cycle where managers arose as scientific researchers able to identify the best ways to perform jobs on the basis of positive evidence, and then evolved into decision makers, coordinators, and political actors. New organizations will not benefit from centralizing decisions and/or coordination, while the political sphere will be severely limited by the loss of those two roles. Instead, these new organizations – which will be polymorphic and constantly adapting and reshaping themselves – will need researchers of a different kind who concentrate more on exploration, as anticipated by James March (1991) in a fine article on exploration and exploitation in organizational learning. Managers are scientists, but whereas in Taylor's time this meant positive scientists, more engineers than creative practitioners, the managers of the future will be creators, and analyzers of social and technical systems.

In conclusion to this chapter, I think that the words of James March are appropriate. According to March, people more commonly follow known alternatives and try to exploit them instead of exploring novel ones, with the consequence that:

> Mutual learning leads to convergence between organizational and individual beliefs. The convergence is generally useful both to individuals and for an organization. However, a major threat to the effectiveness of such learning is the possibility that individuals will adjust to an organizational code before the code can learn from them.
>
> (March, 1991: 85)

4 The impact of technology: an analogy with the world of MMOG

The first three chapters provided the background for analyzing the ongoing changes that will force organizations to be designed in a completely different way. They explored how individuals and societies are moving toward a demand for more liberty, which is at odds with the fact that formal organizations are designed to constrain behaviors and limit change. They examined the nature of the constraints imposed by contemporary organizations, and analyzed how they cannot be treated as adverse effects which can be countered because they are linked to the very identity of organizational design. The reader may have been doubtful. The trends described have been unfolding for a while; they date back to the 1970s, even though they have come to widespread attention only recently. Hence it is legitimate to ask why they should have an impact today, and why they have not done so in the past.

I can use an analogy with chemical reactions to introduce the theme of this chapter. Some chemical reactions require a catalyst to occur. In largely the same manner, the reaction leading to the organization of the future has required a catalyst, which is the emergence of collaborative and digital technologies, and more generally technology designed to inform, communicate, and share knowledge and plans among individuals. These technologies have changed the very structure of human interaction, overcoming time and space barriers, even though we cannot fully comprehend their impact because we are so deeply immersed in their flow. By theoretically connecting everybody with everybody, they have allowed an unprecedented flow of conversations which are giving even more momentum to the process of liberation that I have described.

Technology is the new factor which empowers change because it alters the way in which we can pursue our goals. Contemporary technology has altered the technological plans that we can envision to fulfill our desires and goals. Even our understanding of praxeology has changed. In fact, according to liberalism, the theoretical perspective on which this book is based, technology has a role in praxeology. I accept the extended definition given to the action axiom by Rothbard (1976: 59) where "a man chooses to employ means according to a technological plan in the present because he expects to arrive at his goals in some future time." The technological plan is an integral part of action because it defines the attainability of the goals and it opens up alternatives to be pursued. In this sense a change in technology can trigger a change in action. Before the advent of digital and collaborative technologies, the idea of coordinating complex human action could not be thought outside the traditional hierarchical paradigm. In fact, many still cannot conceive it, given their limited grasp of what these technologies are able to attain. Apart from changing the very fabric of human action, technology also has a major role in shaping organizations, as illustrated by Stinchcombe (1965) in his description of available social technology as one of the fundamental bricks in the construction and design of an organization.

In this light, it is important that we consider how the current evolution of technology opens opportunities to design organizations that allow fulfillment of the emerging basic needs and societal values which I have described. I consider the available technology that we observe in the market to be the catalyst for a paradigm shift which enables individuals to take the central place on the stage of organizations. While in the past information needed to be concentrated because of the lack of tools to let spontaneous order emerge in the presence of economies of scale and other advantages for the emergence of internal hierarchies, today we no longer need to centralize decision-making processes. Information flows have been liberated from the control of centralized institutions or units and can be made readily available to everybody. The problem becomes how to make sense of them and translate them into everyday use.

An interesting example of what is available today consists of the evolution of ERM, i.e. employee relationship management tools designed to allow employees to interact with their organization. Some of the ERM system enables managers to analyze complex patterns of data almost effortlessly, and run scenarios and simulations on the consequences of changes, for example in how they evaluate their employees. Companies like SAS, salesforce.com, ADP, and many others provide the tools, but are faced with the difficulty in using them encountered by managers, who are still excessively conditioned by the idea that decisions need to be centralized. HR functions play an ambiguous role, as I will describe in Chapter 7.

Despite the fact that we might diverge as to how we evaluate the emergence of collaborative technology, we may agree that the advent of social media and digital technologies, coupled with the mobile world, represents a clear departure from the past. It is not that we have no experience of such changes, if we think that the PC became a widespread instrument only at the end of the 1990s, and we witnessed its diffusion within organizations and then among households. However, the changes that the PC brought about were of a limited nature compared to the revolution of social media and collaborative and mobile technologies. The PC was somehow too closely connected also symbolically with the experience of television, and therefore hard to merge with everyday activities. Its extension into the personal sphere through smartphones (and soon wearable devices), and the continuous inter-connectedness based on the internet and mobile networks, but managed through innovative instruments like social media, allow for a completely different experience. As I will try to demonstrate, this technology allows spontaneous order to operate without the constraints of prices and the market. For the first time in history, complex coordination can be favored by the use of light-speed tools that connect many actors at the same time and allow them to come up with rapid decisions, as well as aggregating those interested and capable on a problem-focused basis. These technologies have rendered coordination faster, but they are also able to convey more information and more details than simple price systems. In a sense they are solving the paradox of markets, which could operate through a very simple mechanism (price) but were affected by the problem of market failure under conditions of increasing complexity which a simple signal like price could not capture.

Somehow, the PC can be interpreted as the last evolution of the traditional kind of organizational tool designed to allow a greater ability to treat information and share information through emails in an asynchronous mode. At its core, it was a tool which put the formalization of organizational decisions "on steroids." And its limited mobility allowed organizations to exercise control over its use. Despite the fact that it had an impact, it did not substantially alter the overall design of organizations. Computers made them faster, helped them to identify smoother ways of performing activities and processes, but did not alter their fabric of hierarchy and control.

What we face with the mobile revolution, instead, is that diffused ownership of smartphones allows people to cross all formal boundaries and be interconnected also when at work, with no chance for the organization to enforce its control. Our freedom to be translates into our most natural act as a social animal: interacting with others. Moreover, it means that people can reach out to circles of other individuals who might live far away, thus completely reshaping the concept of identity and the reference groups of which they are part.

A detailed analysis of the interplay between technology and organization would fall outside the scope of this book, but it is important to stress that I am not assuming technological determinism. I do not think that new technologies *per se* can change organizations and society. As I have said, they act as a catalyst, so that the change process is happening for the more deeply-lying reasons that I dealt with in the first chapters. I believe that they offer the opportunity for change by empowering existing trends at the individual and societal level, and allowing them fully to exert their consequences on collective action of any form, be it a business organization, state organization or a social movement. The challenges to the traditional order were present well before the emergence of contemporary digital technology, but they were unable to gain enough momentum and support to emerge, being suffocated by the strict nature of most organizational contexts.

Let me add an item to my theoretical model. I have explained how indebted I am to liberalism and phenomenology. Both assert the importance of human action, even though they do not neglect the fact that human action is constrained by many factors. It is for this reason that they never rely on social construction or on a naïvely positivist account of reality, balancing between these two possible alternatives. As regards technology, this tradition of thought lies at the heart of non-deterministic perspectives on the interaction between technology and organizations. My interpretation of technology in the interaction with organizational design is non-deterministic. I consider technology and organization to be the outcomes of a process of imbrication of material and human agency (Leonardi, 2011). Material agency is "the capacity for nonhuman entities to act on their own, apart from human intervention," while human agency is "the ability to form and realize one's goals" (Leonardi, 2011: 147–148). These two components interconnect to form technologies and organizations. The idea of imbrication is that actual technologies and organizations can be seen as interconnected patterns or configurations of material and human agencies which are interwoven to the point that it may be difficult to disassemble them. From this perspective I contend that emerging mobile and digital technologies are interweaving a material agency and human agency which are different from those prevalent in organizations and oriented toward a view of human agency connected to the emerging basic needs and societal values. As such, their diffusion in organizations cannot fully generate change unless organizations are able to evolve ways to imbricate them in novel design models. Emerging technologies provide affordances, which had never been available before. An example is the diffusion of tools to help collectives take decisions, like Synthetron, a software to organize participatory decision processes across hundreds or even thousands of participants. These affordances are tempting to many who are in search of more freedom and initiative within organizations, but they clash with the overwhelming desire for control of existing organizations. It is common to hear managers declare that they like these new technologies but are puzzled by the fact that they cannot control what decisions might emerge. But this is exactly why these technologies attract them!

However, the power of affordances enabled by emerging technologies is such that there is no turning back. Organizations will change, even the more reactionary ones. The true question becomes how they will change, and in what direction. A powerful metaphor of how organizations will evolve is provided by the analysis of how spontaneous order and organization evolve in social movements. While social movements research has done excellent work in describing the emergence of novel forms of social coordination *ex post*, it fails to capture the elements of change when they occur. It is for this reason that I shall cite my experience as a member of an online MMOG (Bainbridge, 2007) to bring some empirical elements into this discussion.

An MMOG may seem an exotic term, and it is clearly not connected directly to management and the world of business organizations. MMOG is the acronym for Massively Multiplayer Online Game, which is a game that people can play online by accessing from an incredible number of different computers or devices a realm where they can interact with each other while accomplishing the goals of having fun, entertaining themselves, earning money, gaining respect, increasing their status, and achieving many other important social and personal goals. Most games provide the basis to define social interactions. However, computer games were long confined to a limited set of gamers. The advent of the internet and the popularization of internet access have led to the design of games which take advantage of the possibility for players to interact in massive numbers. Some of these games are hosted by consoles; others can be downloaded and used through computers; an increasing number are multiplatform and can be enjoyed through many different personal devices.

The importance of games to society and business organizations is by no means a new phenomenon. I confess that many of the ideas that led to this book were largely inspired by hearing a speech delivered by Jane McGonigal in Milan in 2011. McGonigal is the author of an impressive book which details how we should learn from games to change the reality in which we live: *Reality is Broken: Why Games Make Us Better and How They Can Change the World* (McGonigal and Whelan, 2012). In her book, McGonigal reverses the common assumptions as to why people seem to escape reality to become involved with games. She points out that they eventually find in games what may be missing in the design of their everyday lives. She refers to positive psychology, which has a major role in this book as well, for an explanation of the feelings of self-attainment and involvement that games may promote. While McGonigal does not explicitly describe examples of MMORPG (Massively Multiplayer Online Role Playing Games) and predominantly illustrates serious games to which she has contributed as a game designer, her view is clearly the same as mine.

To return to why I think that MMOGs can provide ideas on how to design organizations, I must confess that I have been a member of one of them for several years. I refer to EVE Online (Feng et al., 2007), a game set in a science fiction world where players engage in many different activities, developing their own characters, and acquiring resources, and abilities through time. Due to its unique characteristics, EVE Online is a particularly complex game to play, and it has been analyzed by several research papers (Carter and Gibbs, 2013; Paul, 2011). Although my endeavors in EVE Online have not been remarkable, because of obvious time constraints imposed by my real life, I have used this experience as an analogy of spontaneous order, and how it may emerge when free individuals engage in a shared space of action. In fact, the game does not have many rules, and even those prevalent (e.g. not shooting characters who have lost their spaceship and are in a space pod) can be violated by rogue players. In a sense, the virtual world of EVE Online is like a parallel universe where people engage in individual and social interactions through avatars that they create.

The increasing intermediation of relations within and across organizations by virtue of digital technologies creates an opportunity to rethink organizations as spaces and multiverses akin to those that we experience in a MMOG. Let me point out some key aspects of this analogy, which relate to the overall theme of creating new models for organizational design centered on re-discovery of the individual.

4.1 Multiple identities and multiple layers of identification

The emerging literature on social worlds online points out that much of our present interpretation of identities and roles may not be appropriate when we address these new forms of social organization. In fact, research has shown that individuals tend to experience multifaceted roles, creating different characters to express different personal characteristics which may not have found a place in the real world. Relations in online worlds come about through multi-relational social networks characterized by different attributes. For example, in their research Szell and colleagues (Szell et al., 2010) identify six types of network according to the nature of the interactions: communication, friendship, trade, enmity, attack, and bounty. The six network types closely overlap, providing evidence of the multidimensional nature of online relations. At the individual level, Shen (2013: 688) illustrates how online games "provide a sophisticated and malleable third place where multiple layers of sociability may co-exist" instead of being homogeneous environments designed for social interaction.

In MMOGs, the ease of access enables players to explore multiple identities and layers of identification through membership of so many different communities. The contact points with others are multiplied by exponential factors, and players can explore who they are and who they want to be through direct experimentation.

The diffusion of technology is creating the context for an unparalleled increase in social identity experimentation. We know from established research that people may define their roles differently on the basis of different forms of social gathering, but in the real world there are both limits to the number of contexts to explore (given the time constraints for a direct relationship), and to the required consistency, dictated by the overlap among the different domains and the established role conventions. Conversely, virtual worlds allow any individual to break free from his/her existing real role, and even perform a multiplicity of roles within the same game or across different games, or even both. The opportunity to experiment with such freedom greatly benefits learning about one's characteristics, and allows development in many different directions without the restraints typical of the mono-dimensional social systems that most organizations end up being. If we considered seriously the possibility of developing many different roles, we would probably have to promote a complete revision of how we simplify the task of understanding our competencies and abilities through testing and assessment centers. What if, instead of creating fake experiences and forcing people to fit with mono-dimensional models, we could really observe different levels of individual activation and help people experience different parts of themselves, i.e. their multiple real avatars.

When we consider these characteristics of MMOGs, it is evident that organizational design needs to break free from the constraints of specific and attributed roles. Rather, organizations need to be transformed in a context where active experimentation of different roles, competencies, behaviors, and attitudes is the goal for design. Allowing experimentation with multiplicity is the future of training and development, but it cannot be dictated. As happens in MMOGs, not everybody prefers to engage in multiple layers of connection, and the share of solo-player keeps being very relevant. Coupling the importance of multiplicity of identities with freedom means that organizations need to provide a loosely-coupled environment and promote experimentation, but they should be respectful of individual freedom to choose whether or not to engage in it. This is not only an issue of multiple identities within organizations, however; in new organizations, people should be encouraged to embrace multi-membership, which is being part of different organizations at different layers. Although this inevitably raises concerns about security and ownership, it is already a fact that innovativeness is coupled with the ability by individuals to be part of very different social contexts (consider, for example, the role played by scientific and academic networks in business innovation). Technology enables individuals to be active members of many different communities, and (why not?) organizations and even legal entities. In a sense this is the extreme consequence of the fact that in a VUCA world, competition and cooperation may go hand in hand, as symbolized by the neologism of "coopetition" (Brandenburger and Nalebuff, 2011). Variety is a tool to increase our innovativeness and to allow individuals to experiment with different parts of themselves, escaping the trap of being forced into a single professional role and model forever.

4.2 Reduce status and social barriers

A large part of our relational perceptions are mediated by visual clues (Mason et al., 2006). In fact, vision enjoys a powerful role among our senses, together with hearing. Studies on social categorization show that individuals interpret visual clues to allocate people to categories. Besides vision, we use information about others to attribute characteristics to them on the basis of which we act and relate to them.

At the same time, social encounters are not as unbound as one might think. In fact, society is largely characterized by homophily, which is the preference for individuals who appear similar to us in terms of several possible characteristics (McPherson et al., 2001). The presence of homophily acts to make organizations and social groups more homogeneous than they would be if they were based on random choices (McPherson and Smith-Lovin, 1987).

If we couple these two elements (categorization based on vision and homophily in organizations), we realize how the advent of technologies which allow people to reach out to other individuals very different from them, and without being biased by visual or information clues about them, can be very beneficial to innovation and experimentation. In fact, a common view of innovation is that it is best characterized by the presence of heterogeneity in the teams which are in charge of it. Once again, variety acts as a resource in the search for innovation.

Within MMOGs it is a common experience to become part of a Company or Alliance (in some games it will be a guild, or a clan or another kind of team) with individuals from very different backgrounds. In a different MMORPG, where the added letters RP stand for Role Playing to denote the need in these games to create a persona through interactions, and not by elaborating an avatar through the affordances of the game software, I had a revealing experience. The game was Star Trek Genesis, a very successful Italian online RPG. The game consists of a set of chat rooms that players can access on the basis of their roles. There is no goal in this RPG apart from establishing a realistic Star Trek environment in which to interact through writing. From time to time, themes are launched by the Administrators, but only as overarching events that help players engage in collective storytelling. As a player in this RPG, I encountered people with radically different backgrounds, ages, and geographical provenances, who shared a genuine Star Trek passion but would never have met for any other reason. At one time, my character was involved in an adventurous action with another character played by a 19-year-old high school drop-out who lived in a small village in Central Italy. She worked in her family's store, a tiny haberdashery. Our real life was not at the core of the interaction because it was based on the RPG theme, but our different backgrounds helped us share ideas from very different perspectives. Using a Venn diagram, Star Trek was the only thing that we had in common, but this meant that each of us could open up completely new learning for the other.

Digital technologies allow individuals to experiment with different identities. At the same time, they allow them to create unexpected patterns of interaction which counter homophily and categorization and actively reduce status and social barriers.

Although organizations have recognized this, the tools used to promote more heterogeneity have not proved particularly effective. It is common, for example, to design training sessions so that heterogeneous people meet each other in class. However, in these circumstances it is still difficult to overcome existing barriers and to give those encounters value in the long term. As a personal example, in the 1990s I participated in an intensive program on teaching promoted by a leading business school at the global level, the International Teachers Program. After twenty days spent together in class with many levels of interaction, I cannot forget what a German colleague said to me: "You have not changed my view on Italians. I just think you are not an example of a real Italian." In the same vein, it is difficult to think that a short time together in a classroom environment can induce engineers in the R&D department to change their views on their colleagues in the marketing department.

Digital technologies allow a greater variety of encounters, and they may be designed to shield perception based on visual cues or other background information on people that we encounter. To do so, organizations need to revise their very strict codes on a person's identification on internal media and let a more joyful and free approach emerge. Why can they not think of allowing employees to create many avatars of themselves with which to engage in meaningful connections with others? Clearly, if such were the policy, people might be made aware of the consequences and the risks involved in those very same interactions, and actively reduce them by raising the levels of attention and acknowledgment.

In analogy to an evolutionary system, these technologies might be designed so as to allow an increase in variety, not only at the level of the identities that people experiment with, but also in terms of patterns of interconnectedness and encounters. A greater variety based on an increase in degrees of freedom as to how people may define their social sphere could then lead to an increase in the ability to innovate and promote creativity.

4.3 Permeable role barriers

In connection with the ability to promote multiple identities and reach out to others in very different social circles, technologies allow easier access to people. Although this is sometimes a nuisance, if we consider the constant stream of emails and requests for contact to which we are exposed, it should be noted that the ease with which people reach out is also a powerful opportunity to increase variety. Relevant actors and people can be accessed directly without being filtered by their assistants and organizational boundaries. This enables them to gain a better understanding of what is going on in the organization. The reduction of barriers to access to people within organizations allows ideas to flow more freely, and it increases variety. Digital technologies allow this to happen effortlessly. Not surprisingly, therefore, many CEOs are opening up internal blogs to discuss with employees and to gather useful insights and proposals from them. At the same time, the continuous flow of information to and from everybody in the organization acts as a powerful equalizing force. It creates urgency for managers to demonstrate their skills and abilities, and it reduces the risk of their developing political struggles and being distracted from the needs of the business. The ease of access also works as a force that slowly depletes the hierarchy and creates the conditions for a widespread reduction of power distances within organizational hierarchies.

An example of how this can be leveraged is the structure of a competency mapping project that I designed for a leading Italian luxury brand. The company needed to redefine its competency model, which was perceived as unclear and not aligned to the needs of employees across the world. The company consequently thought of revising also its values, vision and mission. While these processes are traditionally conceived in a sequential top-down way which requires first involving top managers, and then designing the system and communicating it to everybody, I proposed creating circles made up of people with the most heterogeneous backgrounds possible. Moreover, I allowed each member to use two wildcards to invite two more participants of their choice to work on the project. Additionally, the consultants and the HR steering team had some wildcards in the form of invitations from the CEO to join the project. This made it possible to include more people in the project and at the same time increase its variety and ability to reach out in the organization.

Clearly, as I will discuss in Chapter 6, a major consequence of these changes is the need to completely redefine the meaning of a management role, if still needed, in these organizations. When all flows are parallel, people are engaged in a continuous flow of interactions which are project and goal-based, so that managers need to evolve into a completely different role. They cannot be the decision-makers, because the organization is constantly changing and evolving and nobody can possess the knowledge to rule over it in the traditional, control-based way.

4.4 Virtual teleporting

Like most science-fiction fans, I have always dreamt of the possibility of teleporting as in the famous Star Trek series and its sequels. Clearly, we are centuries away from teleporting, despite my enthusiasm. However, it is clear that the meaning of being present in organizational settings has changed radically. The materiality of our everyday lives in our offices is completely different from what we experienced twenty or so years ago.

The diffusion of technologies like WhatsApp, Skype, or GoToMeeting makes it possible to join teams and meetings all over the globe and be in direct contact with colleagues and partners. It is reasonable to assume that the interplay between these technologies and those emerging in the online game industry, and in digital experimentation with virtual, immersive, and/ or augmented realities (like the Google Glass, Oculus and many more to come from companies like Samsung, Sony, Microsoft, etc.) will further change our experience of the workplace.

Some companies are already experimenting with immersive technologies, like those analyzed by Wanda J. Orlikowski (2009) in her description of the Project Wonderland office, part of MK20, an online, three-dimensional, immersive environment for workplace collaboration within Sun Microsystems.

While we need to recognize that we do not yet know how these specific technologies will change our work experience, it is clear that such a radical change in the socio-materiality of our organizations cannot leave them untouched. For one thing, for example, employees will experience a multiplicity of universes while remaining in the same building and in the same local community with no need to travel long distances. At the same time, at the same speed with which we move from one email to another, we will be able to switch places, colleagues, topics, etc. While we have been trained to move in a four-dimensional space (time being the fourth dimension, and movement being the ability to go back to the past and try to anticipate the future, though not actually traveling through time, obviously!), these immersive technologies will probably require us to think of multidimensional spaces.

It is impressive to see this happening today, twenty years after the accurate description of the state of development of virtual reality provided by Howard Rheingold (1992), which was very far from becoming a mass product, despite the evident enthusiasm of Rheingold for it.

Notwithstanding the hype surrounding Second Life in the early 2000s (Rymaszewski, 2007), its promises have not been fulfilled. While it very rapidly attracted global attention, usability was a complex issue, as were the physical limits of servers to accommodate massive interaction online. However, we can find traces of the long-lasting impact of this first experimentation in realms like health (Boulos et al., 2007) or learning (Kemp and Livingstone, 2006; Warburton, 2009).

Clearly the diffusion of wearable technologies, be they glasses, watches, soon clothes, and maybe tattoos, coupled with the increase in internet bandwidth, wireless routers, and mobile networks are leading us to possible access to portals between different parallel dimensions, albeit not in the science-fiction sense that I dreamt of as a teenager. Or not yet!

4.5 Melting work and life

If we can freely move across different identities, reach out to others in different places as if we were there, the very meaning of the work/life balance will be completely redefined. The common way to deal with this is to consider time as a sequential dimension, and define what part of it is personal life, and what is work life. Clearly, in this perspective the sum of the two is finite, and the two dimensions are in conflict. But new technologies as I have illustrated will allow us to shift from one place to another, from one role to another, almost effortlessly – and what is more important, instantly. Instead of identifying highly separable instants in time, we should think of a constant flow of mingled activities. In fact, as digital technology progresses, some activities will be undertaken by online agents and bots which complete for us tasks that they can be taught to work on. This is not science fiction: evidence of it is clearly visible in the diffusion of machine learning, which has grown to the point of being a topic for management journals like the *Harvard Business Review* (Hey, 2010) or *The McKinsey Quarterly* ("An executive's guide to machine learning | McKinsey & Company," 2015). Machine learning is an approach to dealing with Big Data that embeds the capability to analyze and take decisions in the selfsame processes that are used to analyze complex patterns of data. These applications are of great help in companies that possess an enormous stock of data on customers and their habits, but they will rapidly find use in analyzing information about employees, and quite soon become products for a larger audience, which will use them in their routine activities. We have had glimpses of how they can make our lives better: for instance, in the evolution of websites that provide price comparisons for products and services offered online. Their actual breadth of action and complexity are very limited, but as our ability to program and analyze data progresses, these initial forms of machine learning will evolve into increasingly more intelligent bots.

The evolution of automated assistants will allow people to experience work and life as two simultaneous activities. Clearly, we may have a utopian or dystopian view of this future. I sincerely believe we can make automated assistants work so that they become useful ways to promote more well-being and reconnect our lives, which were decoupled between work and personal life by the advent of the industrial revolution. Work and life are not two opposite parts of who we are; they are two expressions of the desire for action recognized as the basic element of humanity by praxeology. It is how we have designed organizations, the paradigm of centralization and control, which has separated the two. They are the Humpty Dumpty that we need to reconnect in order to give greater meaning to how we use our time, resources, and desires. From this perspective, organizations will have to be designed very differently. In fact, the need to control the workforce and all work processes by locating all employees on the company's premises will slowly fade away. While I maintain that control will become impossible, and more importantly counterproductive, coordination will not require physical presence to be guaranteed. Therefore, the obsession with designing the workplace and the company's headquarters as containers to host most of the employees will give way to the integrated design of a multiverse of spaces, some physical and communal, others physical and individual, some virtual and communal, others virtual and individual (Table 4.1).

It is important to bear in mind that despite the fact that the workplace will undergo a kind of Big Bang, it will have to be perceived by individuals as a continuous space. This means that the design of the interface between the physical and the virtual, on the one hand, and the individual and the communal on the other, needs to maintain consistency. We will not move across different spaces; we will be in a unified space which extends its boundaries beyond the physical world to the virtual. It is for this reason that I am not talking about the augmented reality space which may somehow lie in between the two. In fact, there will be no such thing as a continuum

Table 4.1 The future workplace

| | | Use and accessibility | |
		Individual	*Communal*
Nature of the space	Physical	• Home office • Silent room	• Corporate offices • Meeting rooms
	Virtual	• Virtual office • Holographic room • Personal virtual desk	• Metaverses • Virtual meeting rooms • Virtual office spaces

between virtual and real, at least not in perception: there will be a unified space that extends across reality and technology with no interruption.

4.6 The consequence?

This chapter is the most debatable because everybody can engage in predicting the consequences of technologies, and many books provide more detailed accounts of them, and probably a more rigorous technical analysis. However, I think that managers are not sufficiently exposed to what is happening at the level of technologies, and I deem it necessary in a book about the future of management and organizations to direct attention to some of these trends. I have speculated only on those opportunities which I believe are closest to our organizations, pointing out how they too seem to converge on the possibility of an approach to coordinating our efforts which is different from using command and control techniques.

These technologies are consistent in creating the possibility of a new synthesis of the new values for organizations at the organizational level. Freedom, cooperation, and sense can greatly benefit from the opportunities to engage in meaningful interactions with others beyond societal boundaries, to reach out to those relations effortlessly and continuously, to gain access to flows of information on the consequences of our actions, and the many other opportunities which await us.

While a consistent framework to use these technologies in the workplace is still missing, their forerunners are social media, which are increasingly connecting the entire globe into an incredible and continuous flow of communication and interaction. What we have realized by observing the amazing success of these new social technologies is that we cannot control them; rather, we have to develop trust and design an interaction environment that allows people to develop self-organizing patterns. At times, some of these patterns will be ineffective, some may become even obnoxious or evil, but we must continue to trust in the fact that any coordination technology in the past has had its negative side. This has not prevented humanity from developing them, and diffusing them in the perception of a greater good.

Risk is a part of management, after all. And the advent of these technologies within our corporate landscapes will create new opportunities and new risks. Whilst, as said, we can anticipate a further reduction in the importance of hierarchy and control as ways to manage organizations (and consequently a further shrinking of traditional manager ranks), the emergence of new opportunities and risks will create space for a new set of roles, some of them connected to part of what managers do today.

The new organization will be similar to a continuous assembling of parts stimulated by variety and initiative. The role of managers in the future will be to observe and choose those patterns, which can (and should) be somehow reinforced by working on the environment to increase their viability and probability as creators of the ultimate source of change, which is freedom.

5 A different framework
for organizational design

I have described why different forces are operating to create the conditions for a profound renovation of how we coordinate our efforts through organizations. As illustrated in Chapter 4, I believe that technology is acting as a powerful catalyst to promote change, through its ability to reinforce integration among individuals within organizations. All these factors contribute to the challenge of how to design organizations by making the traditional hierarchical form obsolete and counterproductive.

Interestingly, changes occurring in different parts of our reality are all converging toward a redefinition of the balance between human agency and structuration. At the individual level, the process through which our basic universal needs (Ryan and Deci, 2000) have made their way through the obstacles of the constraints of our societies is coming to an end. Most social systems are endangered by the rediscovery of the individual, and this has led to extreme reactions, which I consider evidence of how profound this change is going to be. At the societal level, despite differences, value systems are moving into post-materialism (Inglehart, 2015), which is characterized by a search for a more meaningful life. At the technological level, we are extending our capacity beyond our limits, so that we can get rid of many of the social institutions which were designed to help us establish social relations and societal bonds, and to embrace a social space yet to be explored but limitless. We do not need formal organizations to govern our complex interactions because we can devise ways to let order emerge spontaneously through the use of technologies.

In the previous chapters, I pointed out how these changes threaten the survival itself of organizations which were built on very different premises by using available social technologies that were more rigid, and in a societal climate which was less open and free. In this chapter I shall describe how these changes will happen and what kind of organizations will be needed in the near future. Some of the ideas are direct consequences of what is already happening; others are extrapolations from visible trends; others again are the fruit of my theorizing. All in all, they provide guidance for the design of the organizations of the future, but they will need courageous managers to be put in place.

5.1 It is already out there

As I have said, some organizations are already experimenting at the boundaries of these changes. Many of them are start-ups, but also well-known established companies are coming to terms with the need to reshape how they run their business and organize their employees. It is difficult to provide a detailed description of all the elements of innovation because of the absence of a global repository of those changes, and of any systematic survey or research at the global level. In fact, many organizational innovation endeavors are out of reach because they are occurring right now and are not described openly to the outside. As a researcher, I have therefore decided to collect and discuss cases and stories described in journals, blogs, online communities, conferences, and in the general discussion among practitioners and academic researchers. My book sets out to describe the innovation that is occurring as a consequence of the search for more liberty in society and in business organizations. Therefore, it is concerned with what has just started or is about to happen. Unfortunately, research tends to disregard contemporary changes because it is so concerned with replicability and comparability that it avoids treating singularities. This is an important limitation, which dissuades researchers from searching for the early signs of change and innovation. As I described in Chapter 1, it is a consequence of a specific model of research. Instead, phenomenology enquires into the reality of contemporary actions and events, so that I can elaborate on a disparate set of resources in the absence of other data. While this collection of examples might be categorized in a different manner, I choose to identify three domains as the basis of my analysis: architectural models, HRM practices, and digital transformation.

Architectural models

An important area of innovation affects how roles and processes are organized and represented. The design of the organizational structure has long been a key aspect of management actions in organizations. Designing the structure means defining how activities will be performed, and also distributing the hierarchical power across the different layers. Moreover, given the widespread acceptance among practitioners of the existence of a link between strategy and structure, organizational design at the architectural level is believed to be a powerful lever with which to orient behaviors and actions. While this area has long been characterized by the separation between the formal organization and the reality of the informal organization, the recent development points to the need to reinstate the value of the individual's contribution as opposed to the consistency of the organizational design. Some examples of current trends of innovation are:

- New global structures: the definition of new architectures at the macro-organizational level is moving toward greater reliance on the ability of individuals to coordinate activities directly outside the provisions of organizational procedures. The quest for a simpler organization leads managers to rely on the flexibility of individuals. In some cases, simpler organizations are characterized by their reliance on self-managed teams.

- Lean start-up model: this is a model for promoting internal innovation through the application of a framework similar to the one characterizing start-ups, and which is taking root in large, established organizations as a tool to promote a different road to innovation.
- Lean six sigma: this is a model structured to incorporate six sigma principles in the design of organizations. Six sigma principles originate from the search by an organization which constantly struggles to improve its operating processes. Six sigma is meant to define the level of precision of any internal process, which equates to the need to have fewer than three mistakes per million repetitions or products. In six sigma, individuals are key actors because they are in charge of proposing how to improve the organization to achieve the goal of continuous improvement.

HRM practices

Another important tool with which to influence behavior in organizations consists in the means by which individuals come to be attracted to, and inserted into, the organization. This has given rise to an area of research commonly referred to as human resource management, which reflects the emergence of a functional area within organizations dedicated to managing the employee–organization relation. The evolution of HRM occurs through the evolution of existing practices designed to manage people better, or the introduction of completely different and innovative practices. Examples of HRM practices are apparent in the staffing process or in training and development, as defined by company policies aimed at regulating them within a shared framework. Changes are occurring at this level, which is receiving close attention from managers and researchers alike. Some of these changes go in the direction of the evolution that I anticipate. Four of them are worth noting in particular:

- Conversational performance management: the emergence of a new approach to performance management characterized by an ongoing conversation, and marking the demise of forced distribution curves of performance management, is connected to the idea that performance management needs to become a continuous process. Central to it is the idea that each individual matters and should be supported in his/her development. Existing approaches to performance management are too structured.
- Workplace redesign: many companies are working to redesign their physical spaces to accommodate a set of different needs through a modular work space where each activity finds its proper place. Workplace

redesign has the goal of harmonizing work with space in the interest of employees, who are provided with a more enjoyable context that allows greater autonomy in terms both of working hours and work style.

- Tours of duty: this approach marks the creation of a new alliance between the organization and the employee defined by discrete challenges which are of value to both and can lead to renewal or to boundaryless careers. The approach derives from reflections of successful entrepreneurs and managers in Silicon Valley (Hoffman et al., 2014) who propose rethinking the employee compact to account for more flexibility on both sides. Companies should endeavor to create challenging assignments if they want to retain the best employees. At the same time, employees search for adequate challenges and are willing to forgo job security for the sake of experience and skills.
- ROWE (Results-Only Working Environment): this is a codified approach to reorganizing how work is conducted at companies wanting to enhance the work/life balance by removing policies on mandatory presence on company premises. It was made popular by its application to BestBuy in the USA where the adoption of the ROWE program led to productivity gains. It has been recently transformed into a structured approach to managing human resources that relies on the assumption that it is performance that matters most, not physical presence.

Digital transformation

I have already emphasized the importance of technological change, particularly in the form of new digital and mobile technologies. Besides being a catalyst of change, technology provides the opportunity to transform organizations from within. In fact, its widespread use has forced organizations to introduce it in order to keep up with their customers and to enhance the quality of work for their employees. In this respect, two important changes are inducing organizations to adopt a more open environment where liberty can flourish:

- Digital and smart working: this expression is used to describe the diffusion of innovative frameworks for work that cross boundaries between work and personal life. The use of mobile technologies makes it easier to define work outside the office, allowing employees to organize their presence on the basis of their priorities. Smart working can benefit from the use of social collaboration platforms and will be greatly enhanced by the further evolution of tools required to be connected.
- Enterprise 2.0: once a favorite, this has gone somewhat out of fashion, but it still represents a redesign of an organization intended to make employees and customers interact through an extensive use of social media technologies. The idea is to conceptualize organizations as flows of information through a network of connections between insiders and outsiders, customers and employees.

While I have briefly described some of the major changes under way, it is important to show how they have been embraced by different organizations. In the following subsections I will describe several cases of organizational innovation which illustrate some of the features that I have just summarized. As will be seen, there are many different organizations involved, which vary in terms of size, geography, industry. What makes them similar is that they are trying to rethink how they organize by leveraging commitment by individuals through a reduction of constraints and boundaries. They are promoting liberty in organizations, although most of them are still traditional organizations.

Spotify

Spotify is an extremely successful company which delivers a cross-platform streaming music service to more than 75 million active users globally. Spotify was launched in Stockholm in 2006, but is now headquartered in London, while operating in 58 different countries. Spotify was made popular from the management point of view by two videos and a white paper describing its struggle to balance the needs of innovation with those required by its impressive growth. The ideas implemented by Spotify are closely connected with the principles of the Manifesto for Agile Software Development (http://agilemanifesto.org) and the Scrum[1] approach. The basic unit of development at Spotify is termed a "Squad," and it consists of a team, like a mini-startup, which possesses all the skills to complete a project and enjoys full autonomy in how it organizes itself. Each Squad has a specific long-term mission and applies several different management techniques like Kanban, Lean Startup principles, etc. Each Squad has its own workspace with a desk area, a lounge area, and a personal meeting room. In the absence of a formal leader, Squads have their own product owner who is responsible for prioritizing the work but has no say in how the Squad organizes its own activities. Squads can take advantage of the presence of an agile coach who helps them improve how they work through different actions, like one-on-one coaching, running retrospectives, etc. Squads are organized into Tribes which gather all Squads working in related areas. Each Tribe has a Tribe leader and acts as an incubator to the Squads. All Squads in a Tribe work in the same office space, and are organized so that they do not exceed 100 people on the basis of the Dunbar number (a suggested cognitive limit to the number of people with whom one can maintain a stable social relationship). Since processes within Spotify create interdependencies among different Squads, the company scrutinizes them with an ongoing survey. Scrums of Scrums, meetings attended by one person per Squad to settle common issues across different Squads, are occasionally held. The design is completed by Chapters and Guilds. Chapters are groups consisting of a small number of individuals who work in the same Tribe and have similar competencies and skills; the Chapter leader is a line manager. A Guild is a larger community of interest which cuts across different Tribes and gathers people willing to share knowledge, tools, code, and practices. The Guild leader is a coordinator who has no formal authority but works to coordinate the Guild (Kniberg and Ivarsson, 2012).

Zappo's

Zappo's is an extremely successful online shoe retailer headquartered in Las Vegas, which has recently been acquired by Amazon. (Zappo's has been a controversial example lately because of the extreme push to organizational innovation. The company is having mixed results, but the founder still holds firm beliefs that it will eventually adapt to the new design.) Zappo's was established in 1999 and quickly became the leading online footwear and apparel retailer. Its overall turnover is more than $1 billion annually, with 3866 employees. Zappo's has engaged in an ambitious organizational innovation process aimed at converting its structure into a holacracy. In a holacracy, employees are part of voluntary groups called "circles," or peers who help analyze new ideas or problems. Everyone has an equal say, and employees are evaluated and rewarded by peers, not by a boss. The system has allowed more people to take charge of their work goals and problems with the purpose of maintaining a small-firm culture even as the company grows. While the absence of managers might promote chaos, within a holacracy decision-making processes are highly structured. In meetings, for example, anyone can add items to the agenda, but this is documented using online software so that everyone can monitor every decision. There are meeting leaders, known as "lead links," but their role is essentially limited to directing meetings according to a set of rules. They also help the circle keep track of its time and money resources. (Adapted from NPR (2015) and (Gelles, 2015)).

LinkedIn

Ever since it was founded, LinkedIn has been based on an organization-employee compact involving a four-year tour of duty characterized by a revision every two years. Any accomplishments that happened before the four-year window are met with support in advancing employees' careers by proposing a new tour of duty, or a new position. The choice of the four-year window was connected to a time horizon related to several project outcomes in different industries. At LinkedIn the four-year window was aligned with the average development time of software applications. The cornerstones of the LinkedIn model are completed by support for the creation of extensive employee networks outside the organization, and by the establishment of an active alumni network among employees and former employees. The ideal type is one where the organization does not replace the market; rather, it incorporates market structures while retaining the ability to maintain a network of valuable connections. In a system like this, a key role is played by managers and employees, while the HR function is responsible for creating the conditions, formal and informal, so that the system can evolve alongside the set of very different individual level decisions that unfold through time. At LinkedIn this applies strong pressure on the organization and managers to come up with challenges, which are adequate and compelling to win the commitment of the most talented, and precious resources (Hoffman et al., 2014).

Cargill

Cargill provides food, agriculture, financial, and industrial products and services globally, with 152,000 employees in 67 countries, and $134.9 billion in sales and other revenues in 2014. I interviewed the Director for Assessment & Coaching, Engagement & Performance Management on the process of redesigning performance management.

> When I received responsibility for performance management at Cargill, people around me told me "You know you cannot touch it?" It was like a sacred cow. It is still core to companies. It is one of those things that it is like you got it the same way for twenty years, and people get so attached even if it is not so effective, but it becomes part of the culture and part of the way people believe things should be done and the other thing because it is tied to compensation it is even more a sacred cow. Don't mess with compensation. I was new to Cargill and I did not have a really deep understanding of how performance management was approached, therefore I decided not to touch anything and study the system. I partnered with an external research company, and I commissioned a study. We had interviews, we leveraged engagement surveys that had been conducted to check how performance management principles were at Cargill. We came out with an analysis of the state of performance management, compared it to what we knew is important in research, and came up with some recommendations. I had this study, and I only had to wait for the right time to pull it out of my desk. And the time came. That's the other thing that is so important in organizational innovation, and it is organizational readiness. So we had a crisis in 2010, and the company was really struggling with the external world and the changes and the fact that we felt we were not ready and we weren't reacting quickly enough or in an agile way. There was a case internally to simplify practices and to really focus on delivering value to our customers and sustaining our profitability and our growth. That was the climate in the organization. And once I heard these voices from the top managers, that was my window of opportunity. We can simplify, we can focus on what matters, and we can actually add value. We looked at several cultural characteristics of Cargill, and we knew where we were aligning and where we were colliding. I wanted to make

sure about how much it would be accepted, and how much it would be a deviation. We did benchmarking, but the companies which were doing something similar were all technology companies transitioning from the start-up phase, so different from us. Their cultural characteristics were so different from ours that I could not take what they did and implement it at Cargill. Every company has to do this work. There is no silver bullet, there are principles that are common but how they design it is highly contextual. I was not prepared for the pushback from the HR community, and according to colleagues who have done similar changes it is quite common. HR practitioners had a very hard time to believe that we had to change the performance management approach. They did not believe research and our results. They had to radically change their mindset, and some of them are still resisting after eighteen months from the implementation. Line managers got it, but HR managers are resisting. However, we had strong support from the top of the house, our CEO who was willing to take some risk. If you don't have senior leaders in the company, decision makers I mean, that are willing to take a risk on performance management innovation, it is very difficult to put it into place.

So now I can describe the system. What we had before was a very traditional performance management system. A very heavy and administrative form either online or on paper with many fields, which had to be completed. You had to have a year-end assessment and provide feedback on all the different fields, competences, goals, and then rate each of these fields up to twelve. And then come up with an overall rating. People at the beginning of the year had to put goals in their performance plan, while many people did not even know about their goals by the end of the year, and it was very separate from work. It was not used properly to create focus on what people should be doing. Moreover a yearly goal was not very helpful, because you probably needed shorter goals, quarterly if not even monthly. It was not very flexible and useful. It had become an event where managers had to spend dozens of hours to complete these forms at the end of the year. The first thing we changed was to say that the goal setting is a way to align your business strategy and your business goals with what the person is working on, and at the same time these goals really need to be applied in a way that is relevant to your business and to the job. We introduced really different types of goals. So we said to the people "based on your job and what makes sense in the business different goals will make sense." We encouraged them to start putting shorter-term goals. The other thing that we did was simplifying the forms. There is a place for the performance goals, one for the development goals. You can put in many comments. The whole process now is focused on an ongoing discussion between the employee and the manager. We did not put any parameter on how often because we have different businesses and each of them has different needs. It is a continuous process of coaching your employee and as you are having these discussions highlight them on the form so you can have all of them at the end of the year.

(Sharon Arad, Director Assessment and Coaching,
Engagement and Performance Management)

General Electric

GE has fully deployed the Six Sigma culture, with lean processes and a strong commitment to operational processes. This culture is still at the core of GE. However, there is a trend toward new ways of organizing, which are connected to how the context and business environment are changing, becoming so volatile. We are adopting processes which are similar to those used by start-ups, where the idea is to come to a prototype as soon as possible, test it, and then either deploy or abandon it. We call this Fastwork, and it is connected to the idea of the lean start-up model.

Alongside this new approach, we are working on our performance management system, which has long been perceived as some kind of a benchmark ever since it was introduced at the time when Jack Welch was our CEO.

Our goal is to make the system more flexible in order to be able to define different priorities and change them more swiftly, and at the same time promote a more continuous dialogue between managers and employees, and among peers. Both actions target the needs to adjust performance to the ever-changing needs of our business. In this perspective the final performance interview evolves into a feedback session, which is rooted in the many different actions and feedbacks that employees have received in the hope that those might have already had an impact.

The project is experimental, because we believe that each business needs to find its way to the overall goal. We are providing mobile technologies and platforms to support the ongoing dialogue and conversation. We have also considered changing the rating system, and we will probably move to a three-grade rating system. Other changes will be to remove any judgments on potential and leadership from the performance management system because those are dimensions which need to be considered by a different system.

The process is particularly hard because people have grown accustomed to our system, and asking to make such dramatic changes involves a lot of effort in change management and development. The process is still ongoing, and we are not yet settled on a specific new framework, but we agree that our existing system is outdated and needs to be changed.

(Giancarlo Pavan, HR Director Europe Measurement
and Control, GE Energy Services)

Philips

In 2013 Philips launched a massive digital transformation initiative across all business units and countries where it operates in the firm belief that it was needed to revamp the company in the changing landscape of business. A key driver of this change has been Alberto Prado, the Head of Digital Innovation. The urge to change by incorporating a real digital transformation derives from the perception that disruption in the market is accelerating, and incumbent leaders like Philips need to keep on the wave of changes. The change at Philips required defining a clear vision and gaining support at all levels, particularly at the top management level, revealing how it amounted to a real DNA change, not just an investment in marketing, communication, and sales. A key element of the process was to rethink what talent would be needed at Philips, recognizing that it would be the same talent that other companies are competing for, but very different from the past, like creative technologists, corporate entrepreneurs, software developers, data scientists, etc.

Another major change involved the way to innovate, moving from a traditional "waterfall driven" approach to a lean start-up model. As Prado affirms:

> Failure is the measure of progress. If you fail fast and early then you will be able to succeed faster. Digital innovation is about speed and is a totally different way of innovating and co-creating with consumers on products – much of which occurs after the product has come to market. So try to iterate fast and fail fast – and if you need to fail, then fail cheap. You can use it [failure] as a sign of progress, and that is a better place to be than trying to stigmatise it.
>
> (www.thedrum.com/news/2014/11/21/philips-digital-
> innovation-chief-alberto-prado-outlines-4-core-steps-businesses)

The process has involved many initiatives at Philips, which have varied at the country level while being under the umbrella of a common thread and mission. In fact, in order to promote connectivity in the relationships with Philips's customers, the company has realized that it must make dramatic changes in terms of organizational structures, processes, and competencies (Enrica Zacchetti, HRM Lighting Italy, Israel & Greece, Philips; Davies, 2014).

Clearly, a few cases do not make for a major process of change. However, the reason why I am using them is to point out that organizations are *already* struggling with the challenges that I explored in the first chapters of the book. These individual, powerful stories talk about organizations struggling to find ways to support their competitive advantage. As I have anticipated, their stories are diverse and as heterogeneous as one could possibly think. The reason I chose them is precisely this: because I want to help readers realize that their certainties may be rooted in less than firm ground. Change is happening everywhere, even in industries where one would not expect it. It is not only a problem of highly innovative organizations in the information technology arena. It is here, everywhere.

While the examples are highly heterogeneous, it is possible to organize the case study on the basis of the different areas of change that I described earlier and relate them to the new organizational needs that I described in Chapter 3. The areas for organizational innovation and the cases enable us to see how these changes are in fact addressing the major issues that are at the roots of the urge to make a change, issues which in my model relate to the endeavor to promote freedom, variety, and initiative (Table 5.1).

Lean start-up models are ways to promote innovation within established organizations which take advantage of the typical approach of start-ups. These latter endeavor to come up with a prototype to be tested as soon as possible and then improved on the basis of the feedback that they receive. When extended to organizations, these models have the purpose of promoting initiative by employees, while encouraging them to set up work teams comprising disparate competencies to help them develop their own prototype, thereby increasing variety. It is clear, moreover, that this approach can be effective only if people perceive that they are free to experiment with change and different roles in the organization. Innovative organizational structures, like those of Spotify and Zappo's, are other examples of the search for ways to leverage freedom by employees so that they can channel it into initiatives within an organizational context that allows them to experiment with variety in roles, contacts, and processes. When we consider HR practices, it appears evident that conversational performance management is helping people

Table 5.1 Organizational change and organizational needs

	Architectural models	HRM practices	Digital transformation
	Examples: Spotify, Zappo's	Examples: GE, Cargill	Examples: Philips, GE
Freedom	• Lean start-up model • New global structures	• Conversational performance management • Tours of duty • ROWE	• Digital and smart work
Variety	• Lean start-up model • New global structures	• Workplace redesign • Conversational performance management	• Enterprise 2.0 • Digital and smart work
Initiative	• New global structures • Lean start-up model • Lean six sigma	• Tours of duty	• Digital and smart work

break free of very rigid expectations on how they should perform, and promoting a more natural and individualized approach to manager/employee relations. Tours of duty recognize the central role of initiative by individual employees who are asked to take on challenges which are meaningful to them. The ROWE approach contributes to freedom by allowing employees to find their own pattern of home and office work. Workplace redesign is increasingly highlighting the need to provide employees with work spaces which allow them to interact and escape the rigidity of the office model. Innovative architecture and furniture create ever-changing and flexible environments where employees can navigate freely, re-assembling them on the basis of their immediate needs. A similar goal is assigned to emerging forms of digital and smart work, which also promote a more autonomous and free view of the individual worker. The extension of external networks to the internal side of the organization, which is a prominent characteristic of the enterprise 2.0 model, is a clear example of a search for more variety through the connection between producers and consumers.

While the above table should be considered only an example, and there are and will be many more case studies and forms of change in the years to come, it clearly indicates how changes can be interpreted in the direction that I proposed in the first chapter of this book.

Despite the fact that I believe that specific organizational design models need to be highly specific (i.e. unique to any single organization), I think it possible to set out some of the major elements that these models will adopt in the future. These elements are consistent with the changes explored so far, and with the overall goal of promoting freedom, variety, and initiative within and across organizations.

5.2 A new model?

While Keidel (1995) identifies autonomy, cooperation, and control as the basic principles around which organizations are designed, I proposed in Chapter 2 to revise them and instead adopt the terms "liberty," "cooperation," and "sense" as guiding organizational principles which incorporate the changes that organizations face. If business organizations want to survive the changes occurring around and inside them, they have to find ways to incorporate these new values through profound and radical actions of change. The actual form of the new organizational design model is far from being identifiable, but we can define some characteristics that it should develop.

The cornerstone of future organizations, in the age of access and in the network society, is the sharing of information and knowledge among all members of an organization, and probably also among all stakeholders, both internal and external. This in turn requires rethinking the assumptions on the driving force for membership and for commitment. While in the past most actors were regarded as being driven mostly by their roles and responsibilities, organizations in the future will need a deeper adherence to the mission by everybody concerned with their operations. The crucial theme is sense, and organizations in the future will need to reinforce sensemaking on a continuous basis because of the limited possibility of translating direction and mission into formalized roles, procedures, and policies. In parallel with the apt description of markets as conversations, I think we need to accustom ourselves to the fact that also internal organizations will become conversations, conversations where more freedom will allow many more to participate, but at the same time will require the ability to give meaning to what the organization is producing at the collective level.

The right thing to do should emerge from the sense of direction of all actors, at each moment in time, instead of being already defined through structural mechanisms. Communication, knowledge sharing, and a sense of community will need to be reinforced through organizational design which will shift from the design of roles and units to the design of a kind of relational architecture which will need to be social and collaborative. Organizations as monoliths will cease to exist, and the network form which emerged at the end of the 1980s will become the real structure of collective action. While a network is typically composed of nodes and interactions, the important issue is to understand what stabilizing mechanisms will need to be devised to make it operative.

In this process, I envision six main components, which will be briefly described in the following subsections:

1. an information, communication, knowledge-sharing, experience-enhancing infrastructure;
2. a role system relying on multiple, stratified levels of membership;
3. an interactive organizational design map;
4. a spontaneous process of generation of variation;
5. an organizational entropy originator to be built into the everyday operations of the organization;
6. a data dashboard which continuously provides evidence of what is going on to everybody, supported by forms of artificial intelligence.

I provide an illustrative description of the components of this model in Figure 5.1. As will be seen, the framework is evolutionary because it identifies three sources of generation of variety, and a process through which variety can be selected into the infrastructure of the organization. The process is evolutionary also because it is based on a continuous cycle of adaptation.

5.3 The infrastructure

The communication and knowledge-sharing infrastructure can no longer be conceived as a support system aligned with the organizational structure; it acquires the role of the structure, in a sense becoming *the* structure of the organization. How people are connected and how they can actively shape

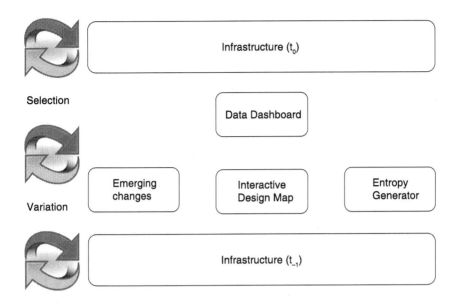

Figure 5.1 The model for the new organization

their connections define the structure and the operating processes much more than what can be described on an organizational chart. The flexibility of new technologies allows a dynamic design by opening new connections and almost instantaneously reorganizing the patterns of communication. In fact, Leonardi and colleagues (Leonardi et al., 2013) describe the Enterprise Social Network as a structure which can be interpreted in terms of three metaphors. According to the authors, enterprise social networks can be understood through these metaphors:

1. a Leaky Pipe, which allows information and knowledge to diffuse across the organization, facilitating coordination, and improving the perception of fairness;
2. an Echo Chamber, where individuals can receive immediate feedback on their ideas and perspectives from other individuals who are similar to them, reinforcing their positions, and;
3. a Social Lubricant, which facilitates connections and the establishment of useful conversations across organizational members.

Given the fact that new technologies make it possible to create ever-changing networks and patterns of communication, the formal structure of the hierarchy loses any meaning as a tool to guide operations. It may survive as a form of description of the relative statuses of organizational members, but its usefulness will be greatly reduced. It will probably soon be replaced, and given the ever-changing nature of processes in the organization, we can envision models of representation which are yet to come. Some of them will take advantage of the technologies that we use to describe social networks and informal ties, as for example in Organizational Network Analysis. The latter is an approach that captures the structure of informal ties among individuals in an organization. At the same time it is able to identify structures in the network and compare different kinds of networks on the basis of differences in the form of relations studied. It usually provides a simple graph composed of nodes and links, which can be made more complex through colors and other forms of representation. However, we shall probably see the development of tools that make it possible to capture the constantly morphing nature of such networks instead of a stable, and static picture at a given instant in time. These descriptions will probably be interactive, allowing other members to grasp what is going on and maybe suggest ideas, or connect themselves or others to ongoing processes. One day, the same representations will be manipulated to open or close connections among participants.

Clearly, the organization will need to think of itself as a network of interactions, more than as a formal employer. Members may vary in terms of the kind of contractual obligations that they have accepted, and it will be important for the organization to be able to establish a flexible infrastructure, which in the end will be the reality of the term "organization." In fact, it must be noted that I am talking about a model where the very meaning of the organization's boundary will be extremely blurred and difficult to define. For this reason, when I talk about the communication and knowledge-sharing infrastructure, it should be considered from an extensive perspective aligned with the early description by Guetzkow and Simon (1955) of communication nets. I am not referring solely to Information Systems or formal communication patterns. The infrastructure should extend to host many different kinds of communication networks, some of which will be private and personal in nature. In fact, one of the consequences of the changes discussed in the previous chapter will be an active redefinition of the concept of work/life balance. Moreover, the extension of the network itself will be in part the consequence of patterns of activation by members who will enjoy greater degrees of freedom in deciding who will join their teams and their internal conversations. What used to be the designer of the organization (management) will need to transform itself into a powerful observer and interpreter, with limited abilities to design, but enough opportunities to generate interactions through the opening and/or closing of connections.

Clearly, in today's terms and with today's technologies, the design of this infrastructure is a puzzle in itself. When we enlarge the scope of the design of this infrastructure, it appears evident that it is beyond the technical domain of the traditional IT function. Instead, it becomes the major responsibility of top management (or more generally the architects of the organizations to come) as the role in charge of defining the overall architecture of how the business needs to be operated. As noted earlier, however, other actors will interfere and provoke changes and adaptations. A key concern will be to strike a balance between, on the one hand, the need to gather enough accountability in terms of what is unfolding in the organization, and on the other, the need to allow enough degrees of freedom to support innovation and change. While in the long run, self-organization will decisively prevail, I envision a transition in which pressures to control will still be present, and will temper the self-organizing properties of these new forms of complex interaction.

Designing the infrastructure will require consideration of different decisions and/or constraints, for example:

- required and prescribed information flows deriving from regulations and decision-making needs;
- communication tools and instruments;
- layout and workplace design;
- desired level of connection with external stakeholders;
- need to make the infrastructure as flexible as possible;
- etc.

Ideally, organizations attempting to achieve radical change will need to adopt solutions that make all of these elements as flexible as possible, so that they can be combined with the minimum effort and as rapidly as possible.

The backbone of the organization evolves into a system of connections quite similar to an ever-evolving pipeline which allows members to constantly reshape flows and connections on the basis of their needs. In a sense, all members are permanently connected to this backbone, apart from the need to design spaces of disconnection required to balance work and life.

While it may be easy to design such an infrastructure in the virtual world of connections, the same modularity and flexibility need to be exhibited in the design of the physical and temporal infrastructure. This entails designing office spaces so as to allow near to complete flexibility, both in terms of the actual workspace and desk space, and in terms of smart working or remote working. The selfsame process will influence how time patterns in work activities are defined so as to create work processes which can be both synchronous and asynchronous on the basis of what is needed, thanks to an ever-evolving set of applications which can support work across time and space boundaries.

Working in an organization will soon develop into an immersive experience aided by mobile and wearable technologies (like Google glasses or the Oculus), which will displace traditional barriers and the still resistant idea of a Monday to Friday, 9am to 5pm work week.

Moreover, the separation between design and operation, stability and change will be definitively removed. In a sense we will witness a constant interplay between change and stability, without the common phases which have been described in the past. Organizational change will cease to exist, because it will not be a separate activity but part of routine work in an organization. The consequences in terms of level of complexity of work for individuals will be extremely important, and in their turn will require a more flexible approach to managing employees.

5.4 Multiplicity in roles

A person who works in this new kind of organization has clearly relinquished the traditional idea of a single role and job position. Employees will embrace an ever-increasing number of different roles which are created, evolve, change, and eventually finish. Roles will be defined by the different projects, which in their turn will activate different relations and connections. In a sense, workers will immerse themselves in very different sets of connections related to different projects, where these connections will be physical, virtual, or both. In analogy to what I described in Chapter 4, members of organizations will act through different avatars, which at times will be very separate identities, at other times more simply different structures of interactions.

The ability to embrace many different roles at once will become a key competence sought by organizations. While this ability will be empowered by the use of technologies that allow people to interact with the different projects and teams, this multiplicity will pose new threats to the need to support people in making sense of the different roles in order to perceive the possibility of personal growth. This is probably closely connected with the idea of moving from a contract to an alliance marked by different and meaningful tours of duty (Hoffman et al., 2014). The main difference will be that individuals will not move from one tour of duty to another; rather, they will simultaneously operate on many different tours of duty and constantly complete and renegotiate several of them in a never-ending flow of action. The concept of KSA (Knowledge, Skills and Abilities) will need to be reframed on the basis of the multiplicity of roles instead of being connected to a specific role. Tools and processes to recruit and evaluate employees will be completely different, and one can envision profound impacts also on education systems.

Managing workers in this new framework will also have a profound impact on management and HR management, potentially disbanding all that has been developed until now in relation to the simple one person = one role equation.

5.5 The interactive organizational design map

The key constraint in these new organizations will be the complexity of defining organizational design *ex ante* due to the characteristics of the so-called VUCA world. When the environment is volatile, uncertain, complex, and ambiguous, there are few things that can be anticipated. In fact, one has to rely on one's ability to act, react, and enact the context. The belief that the organization's design can, albeit asymptotically, align with the best possible solution is confronted with the fact that trends and evolution become chaotic. Sticking to a course of action based on incremental adaptation may not be a good path to survival. While there may be times in which the organization reaches a kind of equilibrium, these conditions will have to be considered temporary.

It is in conditions of blind evolution that we can rely on evolution itself to define how to recast organizational design completely. Any kind of evolutionary machine is based on two engines: one that produces variation, and one which allows for variation to be selected and reproduced through time. The new organizational model will rely on three different processes to generate variation. One of these processes will rely on direct action by internal actors, and it is described in this subsection; the second will be the result of spontaneous action by members of the organization; and the third, which relies on random processes, will be analyzed in the following subsection.

Internally, actors will be enabled to create teams and virtual organizational units by a kind of interactive organizational design map. This map can be conceived as similar to what is commonly found today in online games (for example World of Warcraft or EVE Online), where players can be almost effortlessly re-organized into teams, units, or larger aggregates on the basis of immediate needs. Individuals will also be free to ask to join teams, as is common in games, with the possibility of being evaluated and selected by their peers. To be noted is that this mechanism can be a means to transform the theoretical intuition of the holographic structure into a real tool to rethink organizational design (Mackenzie, 1991).

In its essence, this tool will make it possible to experiment with different possible ways to organize communication and interaction flows. For example, it will be used to call meetings among actors who have not yet interacted but who the management thinks could gain some benefit from working together. Another possible use will be to alter the composition of teams or the location of meetings so as to allow greater variety in how the organization works.

Obviously, the interactive organizational design map will be equipped with tracking software to make sense of the consequences of the various actions directed at experimenting on the composition and operation of the organization.

5.6 The spontaneous change generator

Given the flexibility of roles and processes, one powerful source of change and variety will be the action of the members themselves. Because of the multiplicity of roles and experiences that they will have in the organization's ongoing activities, they will generate learning and change. Among the three processes that generate variety, this is the most complex one to envision because it will operate without any conscious attempt to make it operate. It will be the consequence of actions in organizations to produce changes, which may not be intended and which may have very different impacts. Many of them will be negligible and will be forgotten. This is the case, for instance, when an employee creates an idiosyncratic term or name for a procedure in the organization that at some point may be in use within a larger group but will eventually disappear unless it proves to be more effective. Other actions may even be damaging to the organization, which will react to them. An example is the diffusion of routines whereby construction workers refuse to wear the appropriate protective clothing to symbolize their bravery and coolness. But there are others which will provide value, and will need to be captured and somehow integrated into the overall infrastructure. Examples of emerging innovation usually refer to these actions, as in the well-known example of the creation of Post-it at 3M out of an experiment which initially seemed not to work.

The problem with this component of the model is twofold. On the one hand, changes emerge everywhere, so that it is impossible to keep track of all of them. Moreover, many are not conscious, and people may not recognize them. On the other hand, it is very difficult to gather information on their impact and effectiveness until many organizational time cycles later. Despite the difficulty, it is important to think of this as a powerful part of the emerging design, and devote effort and competencies to collecting evidence of it.

I will always remember how a senior manager at New Holland (today CNH) shared with me his surprise when, as leader of the time and methods team at a plant, he decided to send them out to see how different units were dealing with their assembly tasks. It was found that each of those units had produced some local adaptations, many of which were then of great value for redesigning the assembly process. As he told me during a break in the interview that I was conducting: "We pay people for their physical effort, but by doing so we get access to their brain power. Unfortunately we seldom realize this, and we believe that the only people who have brains are those who work in management or in time and method." I have never forgotten that interview!

5.7 The organizational entropy originator

The last powerful source of variation in the organization is randomness. Given the unpredictability of the future, randomness can be a successful complement to other forms of variation. Because of the complexity of large global organizations, the use of randomness makes it possible to access knowledge and to create connections which would otherwise be inaccessible. Large organizations are already marked by the presence of local arrangements and dynamics determined by presence and interaction, more than by design. To some extent, the design of training programs can be conceived as a way in which traditional organizations get people to interact and know each other.

I propose moving this intuition to another level to create an organizational entropy originator. This is a system that, while relying on random choices, creates opportunities for connection among organizational members who do not know each other. In a sense we can think of this system as analogous to those tiny pieces of software which analyze our patterns of relations on Facebook or LinkedIn and propose a list of potentially interesting contacts. The advantage of an internal originator is that it can create real and formal opportunities for encounter within the boundaries of the organization.

It will assume very different forms according to the creativity of designers and the needs of different organizations. We can imagine it working for example to divert employees from one workspace to another, or to call meetings with random participants, empowering them to make sense of what they can accomplish by meeting together. It can also be a way to diffuse information outside the structured pipelines, for example by diverting an email and forwarding it to other people or copying a document and sending it to other members of the organization. Another form could be the successful approach used by Tinder whereby each member can choose, or not choose, another member to interact with in an endless game of possible encounters favored by the organization.

What is crucial here is defining the extent to which this random disruption of the organization is intended to operate. Some organizations will be very prudent and will limit it, and maybe subject it to preventive control. Others may decide to act more recklessly and allow it to operate with no control and at high rates. Ideally, in fact, this system will make it possible to define parameters and perimeters. Parameters will define the extent to which randomness is operating, while perimeters will make it possible to constrain the random generator to specific parts of the organizations, or strata, or processes.

5.8 The data dashboard

The sole generation of variation does not guarantee the capacity to create an organization able to survive in the new context, as testified by the fact that many mutations in evolutionary terms are unsuccessful and disappear. As I have anticipated, an evolutionary organizational design requires a selection and reproduction mechanism. In traditional organizations, this mechanism has long been represented by management through its learning process across different decisions. The complexity and ambiguity of present tasks make managers a largely inadequate system with which to grant the ability to retain and diffuse successful practices, particularly because what has worked in the past may not be valid for the future.

Organizations will need to develop machine learning ("Artificial intelligence meets the C-suite | McKinsey & Company," 2014), which will run algorithms to analyze qualitative and quantitative data generated in the organization. These learning mechanisms will also be able to generate and distribute surveys and data collection processes on an ongoing basis. Given the non-monotonic pattern of evolution in time, these mechanisms will maintain knowledge and evidence also from unsuccessful projects of the past, which may eventually become suitable alternatives in the future as external and internal conditions vary (consider, for example, the Newton project at Apple, which was a failure but eventually set the path to the present smartphones).

While data collection and analysis will be automatized, organizations will need to open up these flows of data to all their members on a continuous basis. The ongoing flow of data will be organized in dashboards with intuitive and easy interfaces which will enable further analyses as requested and autonomously designed by members of the organization at all levels. I envisage a kind of inverted Panopticon[2] where every single member can see everything and every other member, ending the possibility to use information asymmetry as a powerful tool to control employees.

This system will be essential for the ability to make sense of what is going on in the organization, and to identify those actions which are having an impact. Although its use will be open to everybody, I envision the emergence of specialized roles in charge of monitoring the enormous amount of data produced by the organization to identify recurrent structures and learn from them in the continuous redesign of the organization's infrastructure.

The six elements that I have described constitute the framework for organizational design in the future. They were generated through years of research, and represent a progressive refinement of ideas which date back to the early 1990s, when I thought of an evolutionary structure in my first collective book on organizations (Manzolini et al., 1994).

Clearly, in their present form they are highly conceptual, despite the fact that we can find examples of some of them in action, as testified by the case studies that I have described in this chapter. Nobody has taken them all together as part of a specific organizational model, and this is one of the major challenges for the future of organizations. Designing a specific organizational design model exhibiting these characteristics requires not only vision and ability, but also the integration of technological advances which are in progress but not yet completed. Moreover, it will require some practitioners to take up the challenge and attempt to make these earlier intuitions concrete. However, let me note to interested managers that the rationale behind this model is much easier to deploy. In fact, instead of thinking of complex software and systems, we can envision even a small organization operating on these principles.

The crucial step is the first one: abandoning our assumptions on the need to control and conceiving management as a rational sequence of decision-making acts, instead of an action directed at the discovery of new options for the company. Once we embrace this idea, the tools, approaches, and systems will probably follow. Such a change requires managers with great vision, and a lot of courage, who are willing to risk the comfort of their present position and status only for the pleasure of discovering what lies ahead. This book is of limited value to those who do not recognize themselves in this profile, and they can skip the following chapters, which represent my *manifesto* for freedom management. In fact, unless they are ready to embrace these challenges, the chances of their becoming freedom managers are non-existent.

Notes

1 Scrum is an iterative and incremental agile software development methodology for managing product development. It defines "a flexible, holistic product development strategy where a development team works as a unit to reach a common goal," challenges assumptions of the "traditional, sequential approach" to product development, and enables teams to self-organize by encouraging physical co-location or close online collaboration of all team members, as well as daily face-to-face communication among all team members and disciplines in the project (Wikipedia).
2 The Panopticon was an ideal type of prison proposed by Jeremy Bentham where a single observer could control a large number of inmates through a design which did not allow the observed to understand when and if they were being observed, thereby effectively controlling them.

6 Leadership will never be the same: become a freedom manager

The way we organize our activities is connected to the definition of roles and professions. Just as traditional organizations led to the creation of a new world of professions and jobs, so the coming changes will have profound impacts on the structure of work. I have described how novel activities in the organization of the future will require competencies that we have not yet well defined. Many of these changes will occur as we develop new technologies and new operational approaches to coordinate activities within organizations. It is therefore very difficult to attempt to identify those future jobs at present without providing an account that may prove to be completely arbitrary.

However, one key characteristic of these new organizations will be the demise of hierarchy and control as the key features of organizing. While we have fought a battle over the merits of the role of hierarchy for many years, and Lawler pointed out already in the 1980s that we may need to seek substitutes for hierarchy, managers and hierarchical ladders are still very much in place at most organizations. Interestingly, they are so even at organizations which have chosen to experiment with radical innovation, for example Spotify or Zappo's.

There are many reasons why this might happen. We could interpret it as a clear indication that no matter how hard we struggle, hierarchy and control seem to be the most efficient ways of organizing large bodies of members like those of most organizations. This would be to consider hierarchy as an efficient coordination tool in the vein of Williamson's (1989) Transaction Cost Economics. Others would argue that it is a consequence of the hidden structure of power and domination which is well represented by modern organizations and their internal structuring (Alvesson and Willmott, 1995).

My perception is that the resilience of organizations is related to the fact that they are made to avoid a change toward greater autonomy by individuals. Their very identity is connected to the idea that organizations can be described without considering the individual actors that work within them. There is a pretension of being able to define *ex ante* what will be needed, which I hope I have demonstrated to be impossible for today's organizations.

More importantly, traditional organizations and managers are strictly connected. A way of organizing led to a way of defining leadership positions on the basis of hierarchy of goals and roles. If organizations are bound to change dramatically, can we really think that management will be left untouched?

As a phenomenologist I start by recognizing that the emergence of managers was linked to the definition of management as a science. This marked the passage from an experiential approach to organizing to its definition as a technical activity based on analysis and data which produced principles to be followed. Managers emerged as a consequence of an increase in the specialization of tasks connected with governing activities within organizations. While the origins are clear, the evolution of the role of management has been quite different. I have speculated on this in a published essay, to which I refer in the following discussion (Solari, 2014).

6.1 Management: where are we?

The emergence of management in the modern sense is usually linked to the success of Frederick Winslow Taylor and the researchers of the Scientific Management School (Taylor, 2006), who adopted a functionalist view of organizations. By "functionalist" I mean that managers are recognized as roles which serve a purpose, are useful, and therefore necessary to the ends of organizing. In the same vein we can interpret the work of researchers who provided in-depth descriptions of the functions of management (Fayol and Gray, 1984). For the scientific management school, the function of managers was to study and research organizational processes to identify the best ways to complete tasks rigorously in order to disseminate them and increase the productivity of the entire organization.

Interestingly, the search for a definition of the role of managers and what they are supposed to do is still very popular in practitioner-oriented books, but it has roots in these earlier efforts. What has changed is that there has been a shift from considering functions and roles to analyzing specific leadership behaviors and their relative effectiveness under different circumstances – as for example in contingency theory models of management (Fiedler, 1967; Blake and Mouton, 1964). Most research concentrates on leadership and leadership skills, and it has abandoned any interest in the nature and meaning of the management role itself. The latter is taken for granted, given once again the widespread belief that organizations can only be as they are.

It is apparent that with the progressive specialization of management studies, management *per se* has lost its appeal. The impact of psychology and other social sciences has moved the discourse on management toward greater appreciation of the individual characteristics that make for a good manager and then a leader.

The importance of managers and their central role in modern organizations has attracted attention also from critics. In fact, Marx (1967) assigned

Table 6.1 A typology of criticisms of management

	Functional	Radical
Necessity of the role	Empowerment	Intrinsic control
Interpretation of the role	Goal orientation/ means-end relation	Degradation of work

managers and middle managers the role of controlling and disciplining the industrial army of workmen.

The controversy over the dark side of the role of management has taken different streams, which I classify according to two criteria (Table 6.1):

1. whether the criticisms concern the necessity of the management role (whether it is needed) or the interpretation of the role (how it is performed), and
2. adherence to a functional or a radical approach, where "radical" means connected to an interpretation of social facts rooted in the idea of domination, struggle, and power.

The first two criticisms are directed at the essence of management, and at the usefulness of managers *per se*.

Empowerment

Empowerment can be characterized as either a state of an individual or a process of organizational change aimed at promoting self-reliance and self-determination. When employees are empowered, they do not need direction and control to perform their roles adequately. In this sense, empowering employees diminishes the need for an active role by managers, and ideally could lead to their replacement by self-managed teams. The focus of this approach is functional because it debates how empowered employees can be more effective in performing their tasks than externally directed employees.

Intrinsic control

Contrary to other post-Marxist and radical researchers, Burawoy (1982) downplays the role of formal and direct control in organizations. His focal point is that workers control themselves, and managers appear to influence this process through strategies intended to create and reinforce consent. Self-reinforcing mechanisms, embedded in the division of labor, create the conditions for an organizational space devoid of managers, even though it is far from being "liberated." Burawoy emphasizes how the importance assigned to the role of managers has been over-emphasized with respect to what really happens at the organizational level.

It should be noted that these two approaches have many points of contact with my view of organizations as relying more on self-directed behaviors. However, they both stress the limited utility of managers as sources of hierarchical control, and they implicitly assume that organizations could do without them. I have reasons to think that this is questionable, and I will explain why in the rest of this chapter. But for now let me anticipate that organizations will need some roles somewhat analogous to those that constituted the early version of managers in scientific management theory. In essence, these roles will be freed from everyday routine activities to work at the system level, providing support for the organization's ability to learn. We may decide not to call them managers, but in their essence I think they will be the continuation of that role.

The other two approaches criticize how the role has been and is being performed, more than debating the usefulness of the role itself.

Goal-oriented/means-end relation

From a functional perspective, the need for a change has been argued on the basis of two separate, though related, lines of thought. Drucker (1989) turns to the analysis of non-profit organizations to suggest that managers should change how they operate to provide a different set of values to people in organizations. Managers are in charge of defining a mission and a vision, more than controlling everyday activities and exercising power and discretion. Ghoshal (2005) has criticized the prevalence of a narrow view of human action in most managers due to how they are trained by business schools.

Degradation of work

Braverman (1998) criticizes the way in which managers become part of the process of domination of workers. He illustrates the relation between the emergence of scientific management and the strategy for dominating workers in factories through a constant process of degradation of work obtained by marginalizing discretion and substituting human with technical resources. Managers act as protagonists, using their authority to change roles and processes so that they can make work dull and routine so as to extract the maximum value from it.

The evolution of management has its roots in its functionality to a very specific organization of production. We can regard this as a natural fact, or as an expression of a path to domination and conflict; but both functionalists and radicals attribute what we define as management to the birth of modern organizations active in the production of goods and services. The nature of the relationship between contemporary organizations and managers is so clear that one has reinforced the other, and vice versa. In a sense, this means that the collapse of that very specific way of organizing cannot but lead to either the disappearance of management or a profound revision of what we mean by it.

It might well be that in a few years' time we will find a new terminology to denote a new set of roles which will take the place of managers. For now, I prefer to maintain the term "managers" and enrich it with an adjective – "freedom" – which qualifies what their roles will be. Freedom managers will be at the crossroads between the need to increase freedom and action within organizations, while maintaining a role in directing action or at least intercepting it in order to share the positive consequences. Those familiar with management books will find a striking consonance with a book by the well-known researcher and consultant Tom Peters, *Liberation Management: Necessary Disorganization for the Nanosecond Nineties* (1992). It is consequently important that I describe how the two are related, but at the same time, how my view departs from that of Peters and takes it further on the basis of what has changed in the more than twenty years since his book was published. First, despite its title, Peters' book does not analyze changes occurring at the management level. While he provides many examples of how organizations will need to be designed differently, he seems to assume that managers will still be the same, despite inviting them to adopt a more open approach to experimentation. Second, his book clearly downplays the potential of technology with respect to what we witness today. In fact, the 1990s saw the advent of the internet, but nobody could envision how far it would take us. Third, when dealing with organizational design, Peters relies on a simplified change to the dominant organizational form, proposing the adoption of a project-based organization. In this book, instead, I push the idea of a completely different organization (which I define as the use of spontaneous order as opposed to managed order) to its extreme.

If this is what distinguishes the two books, I am greatly impressed by how early Peters was able to identify the path to change, which has today become a highway, testifying to his marvelous ability to interpret reality. I am therefore indebted to him.

In this chapter I describe in detail the most important new competencies that freedom managers will need to possess, which were absent in Peters' book, my firm belief being that only new (or renovated) managers can really lead the coming change.

6.2 Search for uniqueness

Traditionally, managers are taught to be decision makers. In fact, if we go through the standard program of an MBA, we see that the students are exposed to a basic knowledge of tools, approaches, and common problems across different functional areas in the organization. Also, class activities are directed to allowing them to assume the roles of the actors described in the case studies and make their own decisions as if they were managers. They can thus learn what course of action might be more appropriate and engage in positive discussion on the different alternatives. There is nothing wrong with decision making *per se*. In fact, I think that decision making will still be a competence for managers; the problem is that it will be only one of the competencies, and not the most important one as it is today. I have already dealt with the fact that, as the world increasingly becomes a VUCA world, focusing on an extensive decision-making process is of no use. Too much information is lacking, and we do not have any models to relate actions to consequences: how can we anticipate the future course of action? If this is true, deciding takes on a completely different meaning.

The focus on decision making is heir to the idea that managers are there to rationalize what people do in organizations by virtue of their technical proficiency and observational ability. Right from the start in Scientific Management Theory, managers would be in charge of analyzing problems and processes, using scientific methods to define the best way to proceed, where "best" meant more effective, and in most cases more efficient. In the rather certain environment of that time, this made sense, and so too did the expectation that problems to deal with would repeat themselves in time quite homogeneously. We have learnt that as the complexity and hetero-geneity of problems increase, the possibility of structuring the right way to deal with them decreases. The problem is that when that complexity and heterogeneity grow excessively, not only do we experience a decrease in our ability to structure, but decisions may become so random as to be barely comprehensible. This is no novelty in management theory. In fact, research on Burns and Stalker's model of mechanistic and organic systems of manage-ment (Burns and Stalker, 1961) has revealed that as uncertainty grows managers tend to be overwhelmed. They react by trying to regain control, instead of allowing the organization to react flexibly to the conditions that it experiences. The complexity of having to deal with the unexpected forces managers to search for some certainty, even when it is not of real value to the problems that they have to solve.

In a sense, this is a problem with how we conceptualize decision making as a search for a rational sequence of actions based on the knowledge of a domain and with the aim of turning that path into a structured set of actions to be repeated in the future. This forces managers to transform any experiences of reality that they have into a set of procedures for actions, instead of urging them to consider that they should search for something else. What happens is that organizations and innovations develop continuously, while managers and leaders (and the framework they use) are focused on replicability and standardization.

Decision making under extreme uncertainty, complexity, and ambiguity is a process that aims at developing the ability not to search for regularities but to look for uniqueness. It is not what makes this decision the same as a previous one that counts, but rather the conditions which might make it unique, and therefore not replicable. It is only by developing the ability to scan for differences and uniqueness that managers will be able in the future to provide added value to organizations. In fact, it can be easily anticipated that the structuring of decisions and problems will be more effectively managed through machine learning than by relying on individuals. Individuals, however, will play a major role in disentangling problems to reveal their uniqueness. Clearly this will require teaching them how to analyze complex problems instead of simplifying them, as happens today.

Embracing complexity is much harder than cutting it into pieces; it requires the ability to navigate through different layers of problems, and also the possession of knowledge which ranges far from the established and simplified facts of business. Not only does it require extensive knowledge, it also forces those in charge to keep investing a great amount of their time in being immersed in learning what is happening around them in very different domains of reality. While today managers are mostly concerned with managing the organization or managing the relationships with external stakeholders, in the future they will need to become obsessed with knowing the world both within and outside the organization. While today they can rely on reports on specific problems that they face, soon they will need to read through a continuous flow of reports and facts which will not be directly related to specific problems until they encounter one that will leverage the cumulative learning that they have acquired.

Freedom managers will have the role of searching for uniqueness. Uniqueness will come in very different forms. Internally, it will mean moving away from the standardization of human resources procedures and looking for hidden gems in their talent pools, or hidden ideas and processes in their organizational flow. This is one of the forces which is radically changing performance management, as evidenced in Chapter 5 when GE and Cargill's efforts to change to a conversational performance management process were described. Externally, uniqueness will be found in the ability to identify characteristics in existing markets to which no one pays attention, and leverage them to be unique for a company. An example of this is the extraordinary impact of the drive to usability in Apple products, which has led the company to dominate very separate markets by capturing a value that most marketers did not consider relevant. Not surprisingly, uniqueness is not an unexplored idea, and it is already paying off. In a sense, uniqueness is at the root of all modern views of competitive advantage (consider the Blue Ocean strategy view, for example; Kim and Mauborgne, 2005). In the Blue Ocean view of strategy, companies need to find markets and positions where they are unique and they can reap the benefit without engaging in distressful competition with competitors, which might turn the Ocean red. The same quest for uniqueness can be found in other approaches to strategy, from Michael Porter's (2008) concept of competitive advantage to the more recent resource-based view of the firm (Barney, 1991). Interestingly, while strategy has recognized the need to be unique, and extended it to being internally unique (as in the resource-based view's concern with control of unique resources), management is not taught to think of this as its major role. Freedom managers will be in charge of the search for uniqueness. Their lives will in some sense mimic those of explorers moving through unknown and at times contested terrain to make sense of what lies ahead.

A powerful example of how freedom managers will need to reshape their approach is the journey that led Charles Darwin to develop his theory of evolution, which I use as an example of what freedom managers will need to be.

Charles Darwin: a life of discovery

(van Wyhe and Carroll, 2011), adapted from https://anguscarroll.word press.com/2010/06/09/charles-darwin-a-life-of-discovery/

Charles Robert Darwin was born on February 12, 1809, in Shrewsbury, England. He grew up at The Mount, the family home that overlooked the River Severn. His father, Robert Waring Darwin (1766–1848), was a well-respected and successful physician. . . . At an early age, he developed a passion for collecting – shells, minerals, insects – and a love of fishing and hunting. But he was not a good student. At one point his father told him, "You care for nothing but shooting, dogs, and rat-catching, and you will be a disgrace to yourself and all your family." . . . In desperation, his father sent him to Cambridge to prepare him for the clergy, and it was there that he met John Stevens Henslow, Professor of Botany, who would become his mentor. They talked so often, Darwin became known as "the man who walks with Henslow."

Darwin later wrote, "No pursuit at Cambridge was followed with nearly so much eagerness or gave me so much pleasure as collecting beetles. It was the mere passion for collecting; for I did not dissect them, and rarely compared their external characters with published descriptions, but got them named anyhow. I will give a proof of my zeal: one day, on tearing off some old bark, I saw two rare beetles, and seized one in each hand; then I saw a third and new kind, which I could not bear to lose, so that I popped the one which I held in my right hand into my mouth. Alas! it ejected some intensely acrid fluid, which burnt my tongue so that I was forced to spit the beetle out, which was lost, as was the third one." . . .

The voyage

. . . Circling the world from 1831 to 1836, the *Beagle* discovered no new continents, fought no decisive sea battles, nor returned laden with gold doubloons, bolts of silk or exotic spices. But onboard was Charles Darwin. As the expedition's *de facto* naturalist, he explored unknown reefs and volcanoes, described new birds and reptiles, and unearthed mysterious fossils and shells. He hacked his way through the rain forests of Brazil and clambered to the top of the Andes mountains. He experienced a devastating earthquake which shook the west coast of Chile and explored the tranquil coral islands of the Indian Ocean. From the Antarctic to the tropics, Darwin studied the world's geology, plants, and animals and, as a result, forged the most far-reaching theory in the history of science: evolution by natural selection. . . .

Law of the jungle

On February 16, 1832 they crossed the equator and on February 28 sailed into All Saints Bay at Bahía (Salvador), where Darwin took his first steps in South America. For the next year, the *Beagle* made its way down the coast, conducting surveys, taking soundings and drawing charts, while Darwin collected insects, seashells and rocks. He did not put the pieces together until he returned to England, but it was there – in the heart of South America – that Darwin made his first important discoveries.

Lost in the brilliance of Brazil's rain forest, surrounded by parrots, hummingbirds and orchids, Darwin saw not only the incredible luxuriance and diversity of the Amazon but also the harsh reality of life within it. He watched a predatory wasp hunt down, kill and drag off a spider – a fight to the death between two tiny monsters, a stark example of nature's first law: kill or be killed. Everywhere he looked was a ruthless struggle for survival: vampire bats attacked horses in the dead of night; an unstoppable column of army ants triggered panic throughout the forest. It was Darwin's first real glimpse of the never-ending battle between the hunters and the hunted. . . .

The *Beagle*'s crew spent the second year of the voyage (1833) surveying the east coast of South America while Darwin explored the interior on horseback. Eventually, the ship made its way back to Tierra del Fuego, where Darwin encountered another key piece of information.

Earlier he had seen large rheas, ostrich-like birds, in the Pampas near Bahía Blanca and had heard of a smaller (and rarer) rhea to the south (it is now known unofficially as Darwin's Rhea). Darwin was baffled by the presence of two similar kinds of birds in the same territory. While at Saint Gregory's Bay in the Straits of Magellan, he met the giant Patagonians and questioned them about the tiny rhea. He learned it lived south of the Rio Negro, while the larger one lived only north of the river. Thus, Darwin acquired a small but important fact: species appeared most similar to those in nearby, but geographically separated, areas (rheas are flightless birds). . . .

Galápagos Islands

Although the *Beagle* only stayed five weeks in the Galápagos, it turned out to be an important stop for Darwin. . . . The great variety of birds – hawks, mockingbirds, water-sails, and herons – were clearly related to birds of South America but with significant differences. This puzzled Darwin and later proved critical to the development of his theory. And then there were the finches. Unfortunately, Darwin did not record which island he collected them from, it seemed sufficient to him at the time to simply record that they were from the Galápagos Islands. It was not until 1838 that ornithologist John Gould sorted them out and identified thirteen different species of finch in the *Beagle* collections.

In his journal Darwin observed, "It is very remarkable that a nearly perfect gradation of structure in this one group can be traced in the form of the beak, from one exceeding in dimensions that of the largest gross-beak, to another differing but little from that of a warbler." But he would not realize the significance of this fact until much later. Darwin's Finches, as they are now often called, would become one of the most famous examples of natural selection, but at the time Darwin did not grasp their full importance. In fact, the tortoises provided a better clue: Mr. Lawson, the acting governor, told Darwin he could "at once tell from which island any one was brought." . . .

The making of a theory

Darwin set out in 1831, an aspiring naturalist headed for the clergy, but he stepped off the *Beagle* in 1836 a different man. Before the voyage he had read all of William Paley's major works, including "A View of the Evidences of Christianity" (which was on the exams at Cambridge) and "Natural Theology." In his autobiography (written in 1876, though not published until 1887), Darwin wrote, "The logic of this book [Evidences] and, as I may add, of his 'Natural Theology,' gave me as much delight as did Euclid. The careful study of these works, without attempting to learn any part by rote, was the only part of the academical course which, as I then felt and as I still believe, was of the least use to me in the education of my mind. I did not at that time trouble myself about Paley's premises; and taking these on trust, I was charmed and convinced by the long line of argumentation." In "Natural Theology," Paley invoked his famous watchmaker analogy: any reasonable person, upon finding a watch and seeing its complex and intricate design, would assume it had been made by a watchmaker. In short, design implies a designer. But at least as early as June 1836 – while still on the voyage – Darwin began to have doubts about the fixity of species. In his notes about how the birds and tortoises of the Galápagos varied island to island, he speculated, "If there is the slightest foundation for these remarks, the Zoology of Archipelagos will be well worth examining; for such facts would undermine the stability of species."

By the time he returned, the question in Darwin's mind was not *do* species evolve, but *how*. Evolution itself was not a new idea. In 1809, Jean-Baptiste Lamarck had proposed that species changed by an underlying law of progress and the inheritance of acquired characteristics in his book *Philosophie Zoölogique*. Even Darwin's own grandfather had written on the subject: in "Zoonomia" (1794–1796), Erasmus Darwin had proposed that species adapt to their environment driven by "lust, hunger and danger," an idea at least superficially similar to the theory of natural selection. But these earlier ideas were flawed or incomplete and convinced few naturalists.

Malthus and population

In September 1838 Darwin read "An Essay on the Principle of Population" by Thomas Malthus, and all the pieces fell into place. Malthus argued that human population growth, unless somehow checked, would necessarily outstrip food production. Population growth, according to Malthus, should be geometrical. For example, two parents might have four children, each of whom could have four children, whose children could also have four children and so forth. The result was inevitable competition for resources.

Malthus was referring to human populations, of course – his objectives were socio-political, not scientific. But Darwin could see how the same principle could apply to the natural world. Far more offspring were born than could possibly survive, because there simply wasn't enough food to go around. Individuals with a slight advantage would do better. Over a long period of time, even the smallest advantage would prove decisive. (Thanks to modern geology like Lyell's "Principles of Geology," Darwin had millions of years to work with.)

From the Brazilian rain forest to the Galápagos Islands, Darwin had witnessed the considerable variation between individuals of the same species. True, he didn't know what caused such variations, but he didn't need to – he theorized at a higher level. He contended that the struggle for existence acted upon the smallest differences, however those differences came about. Forced to adapt to ever changing environments, species evolved. In his autobiography Darwin wrote, "Here, then, I had at last got a theory by which to work." . . .

The book that shook the world

On the Origin of Species by Means of Natural Selection was published on November 24, 1859. The first review appeared in the *Athenæum* on November 19, 1859. It was written by John Leifchild. It was negative but not scathing. Next came T. H. Huxley's review in *The Times*, which was positive. There followed reviews in numerous periodicals and newspapers, some positive (Joseph Dalton Hooker in the *Gardeners' Chronicle*), some negative (Bishop Samuel Wilberforce in the *Quarterly Review*).

The first American review was written by Asa Gray and it appeared in the March 1860 issue of the *American Journal of Science and Arts*. It was critical, but positive. Darwin liked the review and wrote to Gray, "Your Review seems to me admirable; by far the best which I have read. I thank you from my heart both for myself, but far more for subject-sake."

Like Huxley in the U.K., Asa Gray became Darwin's main supporter in the U.S., and just as Huxley sparred with Darwin's opponents in England, Gray squared-off against Louis Agassiz at home (both Gray and Agassiz were professors at Harvard University). Not uncritical of Darwin's theory, Gray's main goal was to get it a fair hearing.

Natural selection

Darwin did not, of course, discover "evolution." The idea species "evolved" was not new. The problem was that no one had offered a convincing explanation of *how* they evolved. Until Darwin. He called it "natural selection."

Considering its incredible explanatory power, the theory of natural selection is remarkably simple. Limited resources (there isn't enough food for all the offspring produced) leads to competition. Some individuals will do better than others because they happen to have certain characteristics that give them an edge: speed, strength, etc. Because those individuals are more likely to survive, they are more likely to reproduce and pass on their characteristics to their offspring. Thus the "population" of a species evolves as more and more individuals are born (and survive) who have inherited the characteristics that provide advantage. . . .

Charles Darwin was not content with the established way of interpreting how the world had been created and was interpreted by his contemporaries. He held an open view of reality which led him to progressively see things through different lenses. He was not a revolutionary by nature; rather, he was so afraid of the consequences that he refrained from publishing his earlier ideas until he rushed to finish *The Origin of Species* when he came to know that another researcher was very close to the same ideas. He saw things differently because he had the right intuition and had embarked on a ship that would take him on a unique voyage. Although he knew that the most common viewpoint was the easier choice, he set out to demonstrate that a different view was possible. He was searching for uniqueness, for that element which few people had considered and never brought completely to the attention of the general public. In doing so, he did not restrict himself to his own field of research. He was greatly influenced by ideas from disparate fields. Lyell's geology and the demonstration of the age of earth led Darwin to believe that changes in the environment might have operated on the variety of life forms that he observed. Malthus's perspective on the evolution of society and economy strengthened Darwin's idea of competitive selection as the immanent force behind the evolution of life.

He acted as a freedom manager will need to act: concentrating on what makes for a unique explanation and searching for it, instead of sticking with established views and looking for replication of the received wisdom. In doing so, Darwin had to be very courageous and resist numerous criticisms. Freedom managers have to embrace change before it occurs; hence they will need to face skepticism in their search for a role dedicated to exploring what is unique in organizations. While this new role will be radically different in content from that of the first managers following the Scientific Management revolution, freedom managers will share with them the strong focus on observing and learning. Even when Taylor approached organizations with his scientific methods, he was initially met with disbelief and irony. However, he was able to demonstrate that he had a different view of things which would lead companies to improve their productivity dramatically. For freedom managers, the ultimate goal will not be to standardize and define best practices, but to identify uniquely valuable elements both within and outside their organizations, while their approach to learning will be the same: see things in a unique way.

In order to sustain the development of the ability to search for uniqueness, freedom managers will have to be trained in different areas of learning (Table 6.2). The search for uniqueness starts from the realization that socio-economic systems are complex and cannot be interpreted unless we are able to analyze all the different factors and their possible interactions. In this sense, once again, I am indebted to Mises for his criticism of any idea of governed order, due to the fact that social systems, differently from physical systems, are affected by too much heterogeneity in time to be considered comparable. Owing to the complexity of social systems, the way in which we might

Table 6.2 Search for uniqueness

Competence	Learning areas
Search for uniqueness	• Complex systems • Insight • Inquiry • Advanced statistical analysis

understand them is through the ability to develop insight. While it is still debatable whether insight is something we can learn, it nevertheless requires time to think and reflect on what we observe and know about the external world. Insight is a kind of learning that does not derive from trial and error, but from sudden realization as part of a cognitive and reflective process. Strictly connected to insight is inquiry, as the ability to collect data and information reflexively. Inquiry is central to many theories of organizational development, but given the dynamic of new organizational forms, I suggest that it should become a management competence, and not a specialist role. Finally, advanced statistical analysis will be of help. Although we might devise tools that help us through machine learning, the development of a sound knowledge of data analysis is conducive to the ability to define models of the reality that freedom managers will need to cope with.

6.3 Discovery orientation

Strictly connected with the search for uniqueness as a basis for action is the profound desire to discover the world around us. Darwin's biography is a clear representation of what it means to set out to understand the surrounding world. Its beginning is always an act of disbelief in what we know and see that induces us to embark on a journey toward what we do not know.

While in traditional organizations becoming a manager is mostly a journey through well-defined steps, and individuals who are very cautious and well able to understand social and political dynamics clearly have an advantage, freedom managers will be much more concerned with discovering what lies ahead and outside the common paths.

In the balance between exploration and exploitation which is at the basis of evolutionary views of learning (March, 1991), freedom managers will clearly need to favor exploration. Traditional managers were trained to adopt a very practical attitude to standardizing approaches and processes as fast as they could in the quest for exploitation. This approach worked well under limited conditions of complexity, but it is bound to fail in the future. For this reason, freedom managers need to develop the ability to be constantly in search of something new and unexpected. Once again, this is already present if we consider, for example, the urge for constant change which is the central theme of books like *Only the Paranoid Survive* by the former Intel CEO Andy Grove (1999).

Freedom managers will spend most of their time out of the office both inside and outside the organization as they search for new elements to discover and use to promote change and innovation. They will hunt for hidden gems in the organization by spending time in different operational units, meeting people and engaging them in conversations on the future of the company. At the same time they will need to develop a very public social persona online by working hard to maintain contact with all employees through blogs, social media, and messaging.

Freedom managers will be eager to discover something new and unexpected and use their organizational power to make it real. An example described to me is that of a Senior HR Manager at a leading telecommunications company in Italy who was on a journey to meet employees at the company's call centers. In one of these encounters he came across an employee who was very clear about what could be done to solve many operational issues. Despite the fact that this employee was not part of HR, the Senior HR Manager considered her in a selection process for Training Manager for Customer Operations, which eventually led to her very successful career change. This is only one example, of course, but imagine how freedom managers will be able to move across the organization and discover competencies, ideas, employees, processes, and many other elements of change and innovation.

I envision freedom managers as leaders who are travelers across the organization in search of innovation at all levels and at all times. Instead of being obsessed with the urge to manage the organization, they will seek to revitalize it by creating the unexpected and continuously crossing lines. Their role is to keep searching for the unexpected, and "un-envisioned."

Another powerful historical figure can illustrate the urge to discover that freedom managers should develop. This is Heinrich Schliemann, the man behind the unexpected uncovering of the city of Troy who battled his whole life against the disbelief of his contemporaries, but who was driven by an unparalleled desire for discovery.

The odyssey of Heinrich Schliemann

The uncovering of the city of Troy was one of archaeology's great moments; the discovery of its golden treasure one of the great rewards. Schliemann found it. His wife Sophia wore it. For the first time in 50 years the world is about to see it. Caroline Moorehead tells his story (Moorehead, 1994).

Heinrich Schliemann was a strange figure, and his arrogant, driven and highly anxious nature is inseparable from what was one of the most remarkable quests of 19th-century archaeology, the search for Homer's Troy, the city of Priam and Hector, besieged by Achilles and the Achaeans, come to retrieve their kidnapped Helen. Schliemann's beginnings were modest. Born in January 1822 in the village of Neu-Buckow on the flat, sandy plains of north-east Germany, he was apprenticed at the age of 14 to a grocer. By the age of 24, by dint of extreme determination and a rare aptitude for languages – he was to speak 22 and write perfectly in 11 – Schliemann had been appointed St Petersburg agent by the firm of Schroder & Co, to deal in indigo, the dark blue natural dye from Java and India.

For the next 20 years, Schliemann's life was that of an increasingly prosperous merchant, with an ill-natured Russian wife, three children, and a taste for travel to exotic places. In an age when few people ventured abroad, Schliemann made several world trips, took part in the Californian gold rush and survived a shipwreck. Everywhere he went, he kept a diary, switching seamlessly between languages according to which country he found himself in. He kept meticulous note of measurements, appearances, local customs, food and behaviour. He was energetic and phenomenally curious, never bored, and he seldom complained. If the diaries reveal a lonely figure, letters to his family suggest bossiness and a terrible need to succeed. Satisfied at last that he had made enough money to live off, he abandoned the wife he now hated in St Petersburg and set off for America in search of a divorce. He wrote to a friend in Athens that he wanted a new wife, a young, biddable Greek girl with a good classical education, whom he could mould. A 16-year-old girl from a well-to-do draper's family, with haughty looks and heavy dark hair, was found for him. After a 19-day courtship, Schliemann and Sophia were married. He was now ready for the second phase of his life. At 46, with fluent Turkish and Greek, he intended to become an archaeologist, and to discover the site of Homer's Troy, over which historians were fiercely divided. Some took the view that Homer was simply a poet, singing of legendary tales, while others insisted that he was a historian of what had really taken place several thousand years before somewhere on the coast of Asia Minor.

Schliemann came to archaeology at an excellent moment. The years of his adult life, from 1850 to 1890, spanned one of the most revolutionary periods in the history of science. New discoveries in geology, anthropology and evolutionary biology made it possible to reach back into what Palgrave had called the "speechless past," and to seek ways of bringing prehistory – before the known written word – to light. Schliemann had a very simple plan: to take Homer as a literal guide, and use the descriptive passages in the Iliad and Odyssey as pointers to exact locations. Listening only to Homer, he could not go astray. Schliemann's ferocious energy and single-mindedness made him attractive company to more tentative men. On a first visit to the area in the summer of 1868, he had had the good fortune to encounter Frank Calvert, the US vice-consul. Calvert had done a bit of digging of his own and now persuaded Schliemann that Troy lay beneath the ruins of Hissarlik, a Hellenistic Roman settlement that rose out of the plain near the Dardanelles, and not, as rival scholars put it, below the nearby village of Pinarbasi. Early in 1871, Schliemann arrived at Hissarlik, had a camp built, took on workmen and began to dig. Week after week, season after season, he bullied and cajoled his workmen on. Snakes and scorpions slithered out of the rocks, malaria attacked everyone, owls kept him awake at night, but still he went on digging. Walls came to light, fragments of pottery, humming tops, copper nails, a cache of bones; all intriguing, but nothing to suggest the great wealth of Troy. Cutting shaft after shaft, descending layer by layer deep into the ground, he plunged on down. Not everyone was impressed. At scholarly gatherings throughout Europe, there was much talk of the "romantic financier with the destructive manner of a grave robber." On the morning of 31 May 1873, at around eight o'clock, came the proof he had so desperately wanted; treasure, of a quantity and with enough gold and silver to silence even his most sceptical critics. Here, beyond all doubt, lay Homer's Troy. Schliemann's agreement with the Turks had been that all finds were to be shared. He chose to forget it. Duping the Turkish overseer, he smuggled the treasure to Athens. With the time to examine his find more closely, he saw that it exceeded all his expectations: cups, earrings, goblets, bottles, vases, and two magnificent diadems, which he draped round Sophia's neck. Soon, triumphant letters and a photograph of Sophia as Helen of Troy were on their way to Europe's most eminent archaeologists.

Schliemann expected international acclaim. What he got was disbelief, as it became known that a few details of the find had been made up. Sophia had not been with him at the time, as he claimed, but back in Athens – so doubts grew. If Schliemann lied so easily, had he perhaps not stolen some of the pieces from some other site? Had he bought the gold and buried it himself? Though much of the criticism was silly, something in Schliemann's impetuous, boastful manner, made him the perfect target for men more used to sober reticence. To this day, Schliemann's dishonesty is sometimes remembered more clearly than his achievements.

After Troy, he turned his attentions to the Greek mainland. Though his excavations at Mycenae, Tyrins and Orchomenos yielded exceptional finds – the jewel-covered bodies in the shaft graves of Mycenae were one of the first steps in uncovering the great wealth and power of a Mycenaean age – Troy remained his great love. Gradually the attitude of his critics softened. Victorian England warmed to this small, passionate man in his impeccable clothes. Gladstone, doyen of British Homeric scholars, made much of him. In 1884, Schliemann donated the entire Trojan collection to Berlin, in exchange for honours. For a man so tormented by his critics, especially the German academics who seemed to delight in baiting him, these medals and titles must have seemed very sweet.

Yet something about Troy nagged at him. There were still aspects of his finds that refused to fit into their supposed historical setting. Among his enemies was a German artillery officer called Ernst Botticher, a choleric, provocative man who insisted that Hissarlik was not a city, but a necropolis. Despite two separate missions by experts, who confirmed all Schliemann's findings, Botticher continued to mock. As it turned out, he did Schliemann a very good turn.

For some years then, a young and talented German archaeologist called Wilhelm Dorpfeld had been among Schliemann's assistants. He and Schliemann decided to dig once more at Troy. Within a few days, entirely new buildings were unearthed. Soon it became plain that the city Schliemann had named as Homer's Troy could not have been contemporaneous with Mycenae and the Trojan War. The right Troy lay closer to the surface. Whether or not Schliemann acknowledged his error, no one knows. He wrote nothing down. Forty-five years later, Dorpfeld stated that Schliemann had understood his mistake. He knew that he had found Troy, but his Troy was an earlier Troy, and the real Troy was a more prosaic and modest place. The scholar in Schliemann, Dorpfeld insisted, had at the last triumphed over the gold seeker. Schliemann never saw Troy again. The earaches that had plagued him all his life now grew more painful. In the autumn of 1890 he agreed to an operation. It was a success, but he was too restless to take the time to recuperate. Deciding to pause in Naples to see the recent excavations at Pompeii on his way home to Athens, he collapsed on Christmas Day. Next morning, his right side was paralysed. As eight of Naples' most eminent doctors discussed what to do, Schliemann died. Subsequent excavations, the deciphering of Linear B at Knossos, were to confirm many of his theories. Digging too fast, too chaotically and without making proper records, Schliemann had followed Homer faithfully and discovered a lost, prehistoric world. He was a flawed character, but a great archaeologist.

Clearly, Schliemann was a man of his times, and freedom managers will not follow him in the harshness of his character. However, the intensity with which he engaged in his search is what they will need. Discovery is not simply traveling around the organization; it is a constant challenge to see things through different lenses. We know how difficult this can be, since we are constantly struggling to maintain an active balance between what we know and what we might know. The temptation to stick with what is known is a constant threat to freedom managers.

The challenge to develop Discovery Orientation requires the development of different learning areas (Table 6.3). First of all, it requires awareness of how science progresses. Managers tend to overemphasize simplistic views of technological advance which tend to be linear and sequential. We know that science progresses in very different ways, and this is precisely why history of science will have to be part of the learning program for freedom managers. Strictly connected is the need to comprehend how we develop any kind of knowledge through deep understanding of the field of epistemology, which targets the forms through which we develop our knowledge

Table 6.3 Discovery orientation

Competence	Learning areas
Discovery orientation	• History of science • Epistemology • Inquiry • Introspection

of reality. The background provided by epistemology will serve as a basis to help freedom managers acknowledge the role that introspection and inquiry play in discovery. I have already briefly described inquiry as part of another management competence. Introspection is connected to the ability to acquire knowledge on the inside, by developing the ability to reflect on one's internal states and reactions. Without knowledge of our internal processes, it is difficult to discover anything about social systems, which are greatly affected by behaviors and reactions by others.

6.4 Evolutionary, and continuous learning

Management is neither an art nor a physical science; it is a practice which possesses characteristics from both worlds. I think that this very brief sentence encapsulates how learning develops when it comes to management.

Consistently with Mises' claims against historicism (the idea that we can adapt our knowledge of the past to predict contemporary facts), management cannot develop into a predictive science. Failure to incorporate successful practices at other companies is a clear indication of how results are highly idiosyncratic. What works perfectly at Company A may not work as perfectly at Company B; and in fact seldom does, despite the over-reliance of traditional managers on best practices and consulting "magic spells." At the same time, management is not just an isolated activity performed by an artist who creates a piece of art out of nothing.

Like most social sciences, management is a practice which constantly searches for ways to deal with an incredibly complex social world. As such, it can derive some principles from experience, but it has to recognize that these principles are not laws of nature; they are only general trends and indications as to what might happen.

In its essence, management is a social science in the way that it has been described by the long legacy of researchers by whom I am inspired: Weber, Husserl, Mises, and Hayek.

When faced with the complexity of a domain where experience cannot lead to cause-effect laws for action, freedom managers will have to abandon the comfort of the easy recipes for action that have been so damaging to many companies. However, in doing so, they will not languish in complete uncertainty, with no principles to guide them.

Freedom managers will have to rely on their own learning in a critical way, recognizing that it will have limits in predicting the future, but at the same time may be used to test past knowledge on future events, and maybe learn new consequences of the old actions to enrich their schemata. On recognizing the interdependence between individuals and reality, freedom managers will not search for a definitive answer, the right decision, but instead attend to their own learning.

Pablo Picasso's journey in search of the definitive spirit of a bull provides a powerful analogy to how freedom managers will need to work on their learning. In fact, they will need to go further than the first layer of knowledge to understand what is lying beneath it. Once again, this approach resembles some of the techniques used in organizations to foster change, like the 5 Whys commonly adopted in Six Sigma. What is changing is that they are developing into every freedom manager's role, and are not confined to specific activities or professional roles. But let us first see how Picasso reached the form of the perfect bull.

Pablo Picasso "Bull"

www.artyfactory.com/art_appreciation/animals_in_art/pablo_picasso. htm

Pablo Picasso created "Bull" around the Christmas of 1945. "Bull" is a suite of eleven lithographs that have become a master class in how to develop an artwork from the academic to the abstract. In this series of images, all pulled from a single stone, Picasso visually dissects the image of a bull to discover its essential presence through a progressive analysis of its form. Each plate is a successive stage in an investigation to find the absolute "spirit" of the beast.

To start the series, Picasso creates a lively and realistic brush drawing of the bull in lithographic ink. It is a fresh and spontaneous image that lays the foundations for the developments to come. Picasso used the bull as a metaphor throughout his artwork but he refused to be pinned down as to its meaning. Depending on its context, it has been interpreted in various ways: as a representation of the Spanish people; as a comment on fascism and brutality; as a symbol of virility; or as a reflection of Picasso's self image.

At the second stage of the lithograph, Picasso bulks up the form of the bull to increase its expressive power and achieve a more mythical presence.

On Plate 3, the development takes a change of direction. Picasso stops building the beast and starts to dissect the creature with lines of force that follow the contours of its muscles and skeleton. He cuts into the form of the bull much in the same way as a butcher would cut up a carcass. In fact, he was known to have joked with the printers about this butcher analogy. Also at this stage, Picasso introduces the use of a lithographic crayon to add more detail to the surface texture of the animal's skin. The overall effect is reminiscent of Dürer's famous image of a rhinoceros.

Plate 4 sees the artist start to abstract the structure of the bull by simplifying and outlining the major planes of its anatomy. Ten years earlier Picasso had said that "A picture used to be a sum of additions. In my case a picture is a sum of destructions." In view of this statement, lithography seems to be the most natural choice of media for this series of prints. One of the technical advantages of lithography over other printmaking techniques is that you can both add to and subtract from the image with relative ease.

The simplification and stylisation of the image continues on Plate 5. Picasso starts to erase sections of the bull in order to redistribute the balance and reorganise the dynamics between the front and the rear of the creature. First, he reduces its massive head and compresses its features into the small area that was previously the bull's forehead. By enlarging the eye and flattening its horns into a more lyrical design, he creates a sharper focal point at the front of the animal. Next, he erases a section of the back which has the counter effect of raising the front. He literally underlines this change with the bold white line that runs diagonally across the animal, parallel to the new angle of the back. As a counterbalance to this movement, he strengthens a line that runs in the opposite direction across the middle of the body, parallel to the shoulders at the front. Picasso's process of development is like building a house of cards where balance and counterbalance of the individual elements is crucial to the stability of the whole.

At this stage, another new head and tail are created to conform to the style and direction of the developing image. Picasso introduces more curves to soften the network of lines that crisscross the creature. Once again he adjusts the line of the back which now begins as wave on the shoulders and flows like a pulse of energy along the length of its body. The two counterbalancing lines discussed in the previous plate are extended down the front and back legs to act like structural supports for the weight of the bull. All three of these lines intersect at a point that suggests the bull's centre of balance. Through the development of these drawings, Picasso is beginning to understand the displacement of weight and balance between the front and rear of the animal.

As Picasso recognizes the balance of form in the bull, he starts to remove and simplify some of the lines of construction that have served their function. He then encases the essential elements that remain in a taut outline.

Plate 8 continues the reduction and simplification of the image into line with another reconfiguration of the head, legs and tail.

While continuing to have fun with the drawing of the head, Picasso now erases the remaining areas of tone and finally reduces the bull to a line drawing. Only the creature's reproductive organ retains its shading in order to emphasise its gender.

At this penultimate stage, the more complex areas of the line drawing are removed to leave only a few basic lines and shapes that characterise the fundamental forces and correlation of forms in the creature.

In the final print of the series, Picasso reduces the bull to a simple outline which is so carefully considered through the progressive development of each image, that it captures the absolute essence of the creature in as concise an image as possible.

Please explore this link to see the full images of Picasso's "Bull": http://25.media.tumblr.com/tumblr_lir9tjrGpW1qzemfxo1_500.png

The problem with complexity is that it cannot be simplified as many management models do. It needs to be embraced like the first fully descriptive bull in the series, to be dissected in the search for the essential. It should be noted that the essential is not the simplified version of reality, and that the essential is often hard to see, as most of us are reminded when reading as adults *The Little Prince* by Antoine de Saint-Exupéry. Evolutionary and continuous learning is needed to capture the essential through an effort directed to making sense of a complex reality without over-simplifying it. It should be noted that this competence is very difficult to develop and requires freedom managers to constantly challenge themselves and their beliefs. In a sense it is similar to an extreme discipline of the self through which they need to constantly challenge their wisdom and embrace reality with an open mind. We know from cognitive studies that this is almost impossible to achieve completely. We can therefore imagine how hard it will be to achieve even partially as required by this new role.

The elements to develop in order to sustain this competence partially overlap with the first two competencies, in that it will require understanding complex systems, developing insight, and practicing introspection (Table 6.4). Another element will be a command of evolutionary and change

Table 6.4 Evolutionary and continuous learning

Competence	Learning areas
Evolutionary and continuous learning	• Evolutionary and change theories (social systems, organizations, and individuals) • Complex systems • Insight • Introspection • Meditation

theories at different levels (social systems, organizations, and individuals). Finally, although this may induce some readers to raise their eyebrows, meditation techniques have greatly helped me to work on inner learning and discover different perspectives on reality. I think that freedom managers should connect the mental and the bodily much more than we do today.

6.5 Evidence-based insight

While the first three competencies emphasize the qualitative nature of learning and insight, freedom managers will not abandon the power of data analysis. My view is that while they will have to be stronger in developing questions and doubts about reality, they will need to be equipped with tools to help them test their ideas and subject them to sound evaluation procedures. Evidence-based management is attracting increasing interest among managers of traditional organizations because it shows how the large amounts of data that they collect can be used in a sound manner. Moreover, it suggests that research methods can be used to go further than the commonly used wisdom of experience. The suggestion that this literature makes to managers, however, is to develop units with data experts who will work to provide managers with analyses. I completely disagree with the idea that any significant change can be achieved by decoupling the knower (manager) from the knowledge process. Everybody trained in research knows that there is no such thing as objective research. Research is always subject to conditions which researchers need to choose wisely and to consider when revising the results. While I understand that many of those who promote evidence-based management are consultants looking for ways to reap the value of the use of sound research methods, I believe that freedom managers will have to be part of the research and be in charge of it alongside other actors. Once again, I am not talking about science fiction. In fact, within management research there is a growing body of academics who have used Collaborative Management Research (Shani et al., 2007) as an approach to lower the barriers between insiders (managers) and outsiders (researchers) in the search for results that are both more relevant and more rigorous.

In a world so rich in information and knowledge, it is sometimes hard to understand what really has an impact. For this reason, managers will have to possess the ability to envision new ideas while being skilled in checking the hard facts that they can measure and access.

A classic story used to illustrate how evidence-based insight can be beneficial to organizations is the one that recounts the development of sabermetrics in professional baseball in the USA. While sabermetrics had been around for a while, it was not until the Oakland A's team used it to obtain exceptional results that it gained universal appraisal.

Sabermetrics

www.domo.com/blog/2015/02/the-man-behind-moneyball-the-billy-beane-story/

Billy Beane, the baseball general manager whose story was the subject of Michael Lewis' bestselling book *Moneyball: The Art of Winning an Unfair Game* and who was portrayed by Brad Pitt in the film adaptation, is no stranger to algorithms.

Facing one of the smallest budgets for player salaries of any team in baseball in 2002, the Oakland A's were in a bind. Beane, the team's general manager, was fed up with his inability to outbid other teams for good players. He reached out to Paul DePodesta, a Harvard alum with a background in economics who had a knack for baseball statistics. The two of them used Bill James-style advanced statistics to take a second look at how the team was scouting talent.

Beane and DePodesta set about mining decades of data on hundreds of individual players in order to figure out the best strategy for recruiting good players. Their analysis revealed that baseball scouts were overlooking statistics that could accurately predict how many runs a player would score. In short, scouts were clueless when it came to accurately valuing talent.

Drawing from these conclusions, Beane realized that players who scored high on these overlooked statistics were probably undervalued by the bidding market. He began seeking out these "bargain" players, or players who were flying under the radar of other teams but whose statistics suggested that they would score runs.

Despite pushback from baseball scouts, Beane pulled the trigger on his radical new strategy for acquiring players. Beane bet big time on analytics and his efforts paid off. The A's started to win, even against baseball teams that had much larger budgets. The team became the first team in over 100 years of American League baseball to win 20 consecutive games.

The Billy Beane story is one of the best-known data analytics case studies. Since the stodgy MLB machine woke up to the power of statistics, the science of player evaluation and recruiting has changed drastically. For instance, in-game data analysis has yielded insights about baseball pitchers and their tendencies to throw certain pitches in certain situations.

In the decade that has passed since the A's legendary season, sports teams have been integrating statistical analysis into the way they play.

Table 6.5 Evidence-based insight

Competence	Learning areas
Evidence-based insight	• Complex systems • Insight • Research methods • Advanced statistical analysis

I am not an expert on baseball, but I believe that the Oakland A's story is a compelling one for freedom managers. In fact, it is not about delegating analysis to the expert as much as it is about working together to identify insights to be tested through data. Analyzing and deciding are two sides of the same coin and whenever we decouple them we lose their combined strength. Experts will still be needed to run analyses which requires skills that are too cutting edge to be possessed by all managers, but freedom managers should be able to talk the same language (Table 6.5). In order to do so they will need to be trained in Advanced Statistical Analysis, Complex Systems, and Insight, which are part of other competencies as well. Besides these, they will have to develop skills in Research Methods so that they can identify the correct path to analyze the problems they are trying to solve, and avoid finding false positives (false positives are results that confirm our ideas but are biased by some method error).

6.6 Nomadic desire

Traditional organizations can be identified with a social system based on the control of physical resources. The large concentration of resources and people that followed the industrial revolution provided the bases for the evolution of modern organizations. As work has changed, the need to concentrate employees in the same site to gain advantage from power generation by large steam engines has vanished. However, the idea that organizations are hosted by large buildings to which people go has persisted. One of the reasons is that this layout is connected to the vision of command and control which dominates organizations. While it is reasonable to assume that there are still advantages to the geographical concentration of manufacturing activities, most other jobs do not clearly benefit from it. Moreover, the advent of distributed manufacturing connected to the evolution of 3D printers may soon make it obsolete for manufacturing as well.

The description of new organizational forms in Chapter 5 and the definition of the role of freedom managers point to the need to revise the assumption behind traditional offices and workspaces. Rather than the concentration of employees in the same place, we will witness the growth of a vast, networked, distributed pattern of interactions which are sustained by both physical and virtual infrastructures. As I have described, organizations will become multiverses where people gather and interact in parallel places.

If this is going to be the landscape of organizations in the future, freedom managers will not be in corporate offices but constantly moving around the organization to search for uniqueness, to discover, learn, and explore. They will resemble nomads more than the classic C-suite managers. Their nomadism will be supported by constant movement across parts of the organizations but also by different virtual and physical environments. They will live in many different parts of the globe to be exposed to sources of variety which will be of great value to them. This will pose many threats to their emotional stability, and companies will have to understand how to make the requirements of work consistent with the demand for a personal life, despite the fact that, as I have described, technologies will probably allow us to work from everywhere.

If we consider that CEOs today are already subject to many pressures, and have to manage their lives beyond the imaginable (some CEOs are reported to be sleeping no more than three or four hours per night), we should not be surprised if freedom managers are asked to work in such an immersive and demanding way.

Freedom managers will not be constrained by organizational boundaries. They will know that in order to learn they will have to embark on a journey across different experiences and ideas, so that they will be focused also on the outside. They will take part in social innovation and will be eager users of social media to stay afloat.

The most immediate analogy for this kind of life is to be found in science fiction, in particular the world-renowned *Star Trek* series (Kapell, 2010), which describes the journey of a spaceship across many different worlds and experiences.

Star Trek

Star Trek is a science fiction series set 300 years in the future, in a post-capitalist social and technological utopia. *Star Trek* was created in 1966 by World War II pilot and ex-Los Angeles Police Department policeman Gene Roddenberry. Apart from the original series, *Star Trek* has become a global icon, thanks to four different series (*The Next Generation, Deep Space Nine, Voyager,* and *Enterprise*), which have aired at different times, and nine major motion pictures. The connection between the different series and movies is the fact that they portray the intergalactic adventures of various crews of Star Fleet Command space-faring vehicles or orbital station as they traverse the universe exploring strange new worlds and seeking out new life and new civilizations. Each of the series had a different common theme. While the original one set out the boundaries of the *Star Trek* universe, *The Next Generation* followed, adding complexity to it. The original series was centered around Kirk and his crew. *The Next Generation* was also centered around the Enterprise and her captain, but the theme was geared toward the scientific explanations of the universe making it larger in scope.

Deep Space Nine's Dominion War had brought the complex political and interpersonal dynamics between *Star Trek's* various alien cultures to a rousing crescendo, while *Voyager's* particular fondness for dizzyingly high-concept plots had blurred the line between 24th century technology and outright magic.

The central theme of *Star Trek* is nomadic, as different crews explore the universe in a relentless search for what is next. While from time to time most of them touch base on Earth (with the exception of the Voyager which is lost in a parallel quadrant and desperately searches for a way home), most of the action is directed to the unexplored, as clearly stated by the famous opening claim "to boldly go where no man has gone before."

The constant search for another place to visit in *Star Trek* is closely connected to how freedom managers have been described in this chapter, and it appears the best way to conclude it. Freedom managers are experimenters who cannot stay in their offices simply to manage the flow of the organization's decisions. They are there to challenge established ways of doing things. In order to do so, however, they need to constantly engage with new phenomena. From this perspective they become more similar to nomads who wander across different environments, developing constant learning about them, but at the same time experiencing constant changes and adaptations. In a global world, this creates important expectations as to the competencies that freedom managers need to develop. Some of these are connected to the need to reach out to the variety of cultures and experiences that humanity has developed. Despite the fact that English has developed into a *lingua franca*, appreciating the subtleties and the differences which make for the unique requires freedom managers to be trained in various languages and cultures. They will need to speak as many languages as they can, and possess knowledge of the history and habits of many different places. This will be obtained not only through formal training but also by developing an active policy of multilocation whereby their residences will constantly move across the globe.

In order to overcome the bewilderment caused by these experiences, freedom managers will be taught to understand globalization and its forces, by developing knowledge in the domain of cultural and philosophical anthropology. The complexity of differences among cultures will require them to develop a more profound comprehension of the reality they will experience (Table 6.6).

Table 6.6 Nomadic desire

Competence	Learning areas
Nomadic desire	• Languages • Cultural and philosophical anthropology • Globalization • Multilocation

6.7 Freedom managers

This chapter has led you through a journey on how managers will need to change. I have no claims that my account of the new competencies and the emerging roles is complete. I am sure there is much to add, and I am looking forward to discussing it with you on social media and the blogs that will originate from the platform represented by this book. Even more will emerge as we observe the many events and changes in the years to come. However, I am confident that the list of competencies that I have described will be part of the toolbox of freedom managers.

For ease of use, I summarize the different tables in a conclusive one (Table 6.7).

Table 6.7 The competencies of freedom managers

Competence	Learning areas
Search for uniqueness	• Complex systems • Insight • Inquiry • Advanced statistical analysis
Discovery orientation	• History of science • Epistemology • Inquiry • Introspection
Evolutionary and continuous learning	• Evolutionary and change theories (social systems, organizations, and individuals) • Complex systems • Insight • Introspection • Meditation
Evidence-based insight	• Complex systems • Insight • Research methods • Advanced statistical analysis
Nomadic desire	• Languages • Cultural and philosophical anthropology • Globalization • Multilocation

Developing these competencies is not easy, because there are still no formal education programs which target all of them. Moreover, traditional training and development in companies is not structured to take on the challenge of guiding managers through so many topics. There is a need for profound reflection within business schools, and in our education systems, as to how we define training for management-related roles in the future.

While the target is the development of the new freedom managers, many of the competencies that they will need can be considered building blocks of the workforce of the future.

Once I have designed the framework of the coming paradigm change, I think it important to focus on what needs to be done by defining a roadmap for change. However, given the complexity of the changes, instead of one roadmap, I will describe three. The first roadmap is related to you personally, and your role. As I have stated repeatedly, a change to become freedom managers requires courage and the willingness to embrace a radically different view of your role. So before even considering a change in your organization you need to make sure that you are ready for it, and take your colleagues through the same process of acknowledgment. The second roadmap is for your organization. Developing a traditional organization into a new one is akin to a metamorphosis. I am not talking about incremental fixes or patches, but a radical rethinking of the entire organization which will encounter much resistance that you need to prepare for. The third, and final, roadmap extends further than the boundaries of your company because, as we have seen, some of the changes implied stretch well beyond companies. Moreover, it might well be that you are not a manager, but a social and political architect, or in general you want to help your community get ready for the change. So this last roadmap will help you focus some actions required to deal with the future.

7 Getting ready: three roadmaps

In the previous chapters I have described the foundations and the path of a coming change in how we will design and manage the organizations of the future, and most probably our society, given the importance of organizations within it. Clearly, I have elaborated on some recognized trends, but I have also directed attention to forces which are less evident but very strong in forging our future. I hope that you as my reader have by now understood the urgency of change because the time to get prepared is running out.

The foundation of the book is the longstanding tension between individual liberty and the constraints imposed by how we organize socialized activities. The liberation of the individual has been a contested process, but we should recognize that on the timescale of humanity, the three hundred years that separate us from the dawn of humanism represent a very limited span of time. My contention in this book is that the process is accelerating, despite the apparently contradictory evidence of the events at global level that occurred while I was writing it in 2015.

As humanity broke free from the self-imposed chains of tradition and myth, it started a process of liberation which required a constant battle with the impositions of social life rooted in traditional forces which had reigned for thousands of years. While I hold liberty in high regard, I have to admit that it comes with a great responsibility, and with the need to assign everybody a more important role in defining what should happen to themselves. For many years, freedom's appeal to humanity has been countered by the responsibility that it imposes on everybody. The real question, therefore, is whether we are finally ready to embrace the decisive stage of such a change; and I believe that it is business organizations which are best positioned to make it finally flourish.

A clear example of this prominent role is the impact that business organizations have had in legitimizing the idea that everybody should be set free to express their ideas, preferences, and religions. Even within the most repressive regimes, business organizations are creating internal contexts that promote diversity and inclusion, and disseminate ideas of freedom and responsibility very different from those of traditional and even authoritarian societies.

Interestingly, whilst the question of whether we need to rule through direct intervention (visible hand) or let spontaneous order rule (invisible hand) has been a key issue in economics, within management and organization theory it seems to have been largely neglected. In the presence of a growing number of researchers who are addressing management principles from the radical standpoint, attributing to traditional management studies a role in the construction and maintenance of a specific social order, I embrace the perspective of liberalism as the foundation of a different type of criticism. While many radical scholars accuse business organizations of actively constraining and controlling employees on the basis of a dominance agenda rooted in capitalism, and which is connected to neo-liberal economic policies, I interpret the same lack of freedom in organizations as the demise of the ideal of individual liberty and call for a renewed effort to install a liberal agenda not only in the market but also within the boundaries of organizations. While the target is the same (the traditional organization), the process envisioned is very different. Theirs (of the radical scholars) is a process of power confrontation along the lines of modern class identification (for example through the gender, nationality, immigration stratification variables); mine is the complete demise of the over-socialization and structuration of members of any social context in favor of recognition of the inevitable and irrefutable diversity which characterizes each of us individually and resists any form of social categorization, be it mainstream or radical. It is a pity that we lost Michel Foucault so early, because despite the fact that he initially conducted a critique of society very much in line with the Marxian heritage, his last cycle of lectures raised the real question of how to set individuals free without constraining them within a class. Ideally, this is exactly my attack on traditional, formal organizations and their disdain for liberty.

It should be noted that, despite their ideological distance, I have found a striking parallelism between traditional management approaches and so-called "radical" ones in the fact that both give up the individual *per se* in favor of the individual as part of a category. In doing so, they erase from management its essential element, which is the heterogeneity of individuals in any social context. Instead of looking for ways to categorize diversity in classes (or groups), I propose considering diversity at its roots by recognizing that each of us is so diverse as to demand being treated differently for what we are, and not for what we represent to an external observer. Whether this external observer is driven by a command-and-control agenda or by a desire for justice and equality makes no difference to me: traditionalists and radicals are both conservative in this respect. They both neglect the foundational values of individuals within societies, and superimpose their categorization variables on our irreducible uniqueness. In fact, on closer scrutiny both views continue the process of objectification of human beings so well described by Foucault (1995). According to Foucault, a key characteristic of modernity has been its classification and codification of individuals on the basis of objective and measurable features which enable their treatment as subjects by way of the use of different disciplines, which can be interpreted as ways of dissecting individuals into observable entities. Although many radical theorists are familiar with Foucault's analysis, they fail to realize that it also applies to how they interpret society and organizations. Whilst worried by the prospect that the social system and organizations can limit and theoretically remove individuality and liberty from our everyday experience, I do not think that they can be regained through a critical analysis which is internal to the selfsame system that it purports to change. Rather, I firmly believe that social systems need to be crafted as means to empower individuals through levels of cooperation, and not as tools to control and make them subjects or classify them in categories, which is another way of making them subjects.

A consequence of this perspective, as illustrated in this book, is that the liberation of individuals is a process with far-reaching consequences not only within organizations but throughout society. A driver of this change is the emergence of a different approach to what is labeled "management." Despite the fact that it departs markedly from the classic descriptions of leadership and management, I have coined the term "freedom management" to describe the nature of the forthcoming change. I am sure that we will soon devise a better label, one which reflects the fact that organizations and social systems cannot be managed, but at most comprehended in their spontaneous change from one form of spontaneous order to the next. In fact, freedom managers, in analogy with science-fiction movies, may be more adequately described as actors in the process of liberation from the too many constraints that organizations and societies have imposed on the free will and entrepreneurship of individuals. Once this process is completed, we will probably need individuals willing to assume the role of wanderers and roamers through the multiple layers of coordinated social interaction that we will define as organizations. However, calling them managers, even if preceded by the term "freedom," will probably not suit their role.

I believe that this change is already apparent in organizations and social systems at a global level, but we are still far from seeing it unfold as a real shift in society. Exercises in anticipating what it will mean abound, and they vary in terms of their implicit evaluations (Bauman, 2000; Sennett, 2000; Gratton, 2011). I urge you as a leader or manager or organizational activist to understand how many levels will need to be activated to accomplish the transition to this new order. Consistently with my belief in individuals, I start by asking you to reflect on yourself and what you need to change, and then consider the implications for your organization and the wider societal system.

7.1 I need to change

Becoming a freedom manager is not easy. In fact, those who embrace this change will have to consider that they will be on the edge between the old and new landscape of the organization. A change like the one I have described cannot happen overnight; it will require commitment to a long and complex transition. You will risk losing a great deal if you are a traditional manager or organizational leader. Trusting others in their daily activities is already a challenge, as exemplified by many books on how hard it is to delegate successfully. Imagine how hard it will be to start designing an organization where you need to rely on others for so many different activities and at the same time completely change your role engaging in the behaviors required by the new competencies described in Chapter 6. At the same time, you will have to run the business as usual until the organization is ready to transition completely to the new model.

For the transition to be successful, therefore, you will need courage and stamina.

a. Evaluate your freedom manager competencies

The various competencies described in Chapter 6 are a good basis to start from, in identifying what steps you will need to take to develop your personal ability to act as a freedom manager. The first step is to understand where you start from, through a self-reflection, based on your experience and your previous education.

Table 7.1 summarizes the different competencies and provides a way to evaluate your proficiency in each of them. I suggest that you go back to Chapter 6 and read the paragraph on each of the competencies, and then return to this table and try to evaluate yourself as objectively as possible. This exercise can be useful also at the collective level, i.e. performing it with all the top management team. Doing so will allow you to take advantage of the feedback from others and leverage existing complementarities among top management team members

My suggestion is not to reach a judgment based only on perceptions. Try to think of times when you have had a chance to work on these competencies or the learning areas that pertain to them. It can be useful also to understand how you spend your time. Make a note on, or write a brief description of, actual times and events that come to your mind. When doing so you can also think of occasions when you could develop your competencies in the future.

Once you have gone through the five competencies, identify which of them are those on which you score highest, and those on which you appear to lag behind. This ordering will be key for defining how to schedule your time and agenda.

Imagine that you score poorly on "Search for uniqueness." This means that you have to devote a larger amount of your time to strengthening it. This can be accomplished in various ways. You might attend formal classes on some of the learning areas. For example, search for a program on complex systems, and attend it regularly. Some of these programs are available online at sources like Coursera or Kahn Academy. I suggest pairing education with

Table 7.1 Self-evaluation

Competence	Learning areas	Low	Medium	High
Search for uniqueness	• Complex systems • Insight • Inquiry • Advanced statistical analysis			
Discovery orientation	• History of science • Epistemology • Inquiry • Introspection			
Evolutionary and continuous learning	• Evolutionary and change theories (social systems, organizations, and individuals) • Complex systems • Insight • Introspection • Meditation			
Evidence-based insight	• Complex systems • Insight • Research methods • Advanced statistical analysis			
Nomadic desire	• Languages • Cultural and philosophical anthropology • Globalization • Multilocation			

experience, and making sure that you spend at least one hour per day reflecting on one of the learning areas and trying to experience it. You can also rely on expert advice by setting up meetings with key individuals who can help you in the various areas, and establishing a mentoring relationship with them.

The purpose of this first activity is to help you realize how much of what is needed may be already part of your background as a manager. The problem is that you are not nurturing it systematically, whereas you should consider it a priority for your future. Another consequence of this activity is that it promotes a more accurate description of the development plan that you have to set for yourself. Unlike the traditional training and development offered by most organizations, this plan is yours from the outset; it is your personal plan to develop yourself into a freedom manager.

b. Redesign your daily agenda

As you reach a better understanding of what your priorities should be, you have the chance to connect them to how you schedule your time and activities. In fact, while some of the learning areas for the competencies will require some kind of formal training and support, others can be experienced by finding time in your busy schedule to dedicate yourself to them. For example, insight is present in three different competencies. While insight can be better understood by learning the basic elements that generate it, the key is to live through it as a way to experience your daily activity. However, to do so your schedule needs to incorporate enough time free from other appointments and activities, time which can therefore be dedicated to developing your insight even further. Once you have created space for it, it will become easier to elaborate on some new ideas and see them from different angles, or immerse yourself in a book on the triggers of insight.

The reason why I am not providing a structured schedule for you is that I believe in individual liberty. Each of us is different, and we need to find our own ways to deal with the coming changes. What we can benefit from is knowing what processes might help us develop an effective approach to change, but the specific nature of the actions to be undertaken should be part of our idiosyncratic experience.

However, your schedule will have to allocate specific times and places to all five competencies, with more intense dedication to those in which you perceive you need to invest more.

c. Embrace variety

As we have seen, a cornerstone of the organizations of the future will be variety. Variety can arise from various sources. Clearly, for social beings like ourselves, a powerful source is the variety of encounters that we have with people different from us. This is very challenging within organizations because, as we have seen, our organizations and social groups tend to be characterized by homophily: the tendency to associate with similar people. To embrace variety you should be consistent in trying to meet different people in the organization or in other organizations. Walk around your building, and visit different branches to be immersed in the lives of the others. Take somebody whom you randomly choose for a coffee, and an unexpected conversation will follow. I find that an interesting example of this is the TV program *Undercover Boss* by CBS, despite the fact that it is heavily adapted to the format of reality shows. The program describes the experience of CEOs at companies who, thanks to a made-up character, can interact with employees at different levels and in different jobs without being recognized. The TV show is full of drama, but it usually portrays CEOs who were completely unaware of the everyday reality that people experience in their companies. Embracing this attitude is a way to gain a better understanding of what is going on, and also to identify the many talented people that work in the organization but may not be noticed by top managers or HR managers. The same attitude should lead to organizing random encounters at other companies and outside the organization.

Another way to embrace variety is by changing your everyday habits. Challenging our routines can be cumbersome because we have developed them as forms of adaptation to our external world. However, this is another powerful form of variety. Try randomly changing the time when you arrive at the office or take your lunch break and be attentive to what you find different in the people you encounter, in your internal states, and in what you observe around you. We frequently experience the world through the timing of our daily activities. The same coffee shop at 7am will be very different at 11am. This is true of any social and physical environment that you experience, both inside and outside your organization. Overcoming the barriers that come from many years of adaptation may not be easy, but I guarantee that it will provide many new stimuli if you are willing to observe what differences are out there. Finally, another source of variety is attendance at events and visits to places far from those to which we are accustomed. Attending a play, which would never be your first choice allows you to meet people that you might otherwise never encounter. I do the same with books. I search for books which I am sure that I will not like, and then make a point of reading them. This happened for the first time when I was in my teens and stumbled across an excerpt from *In Search of Lost Time* by Marcel Proust. I hated it, from the very moment my middle-school teacher had us read it. I could not understand why she was so passionate about the lengthy (and to me back then quite pointless) description of the reaction to the smell of a madeleine. Initially, with the spontaneous arrogance of an adolescent, I dismissed Proust as a boring writer. But I then realized that even if my reaction was bad, it was symptomatic of something interesting, and I set out to read the entire book (an impressive feat for those familiar with its length). It taught me so much of what I had not yet realized in my twelve years on Earth. And it occurred again with the likes of Honoré de Balzac and Ernest Hemingway, to cite two other prominent writers.

d. Look for mentorship

"No man is an island" is a phrase that accompanies any description of why individuals are at the core of our society. In fact, stressing the need to liberate individuals does not mean neglecting the importance for our development of a network of relations with others. It is precisely because we recognize others that we can make sense of who we are in a constant process of nego-tiating our identity. As individuals, we create bonds with other individuals, and we struggle to maintain them while recognizing that there will always be differences between ourselves and them.

The changes which we undergo in our lives are always interconnected with our network of relations. When we need to make a dramatic change in how we behave, like the change required to become a freedom manager, we may find ourselves in need of support and help from the outside. Another step in the process is therefore to look for mentors who can help us focus our energy in developing the new competencies and attitudes that will be required.

Given the specific nature of the implied change, there are two possible alternatives to explore. On the one hand, it will be beneficial to look for people who are far from our normal circle of acquaintances and who thrive on innovation and change. A clear example of how these people can be helpful, and are already used in organizations, is the success of speakers who share their extreme adventures with business leaders on many company programs. I have personally made frequent use of the YouTube video where Ueli Steck, a Swiss professional climber, describes what he felt when he speed-climbed the Eiger Peak in the Swiss Alps and established a new record. The kind of challenges that a lone climber faces can be very inspirational for a manager embracing a radical change. As Ueli explains, it takes a great deal of preparation, but once you start there is no turning back. As he explains all of a sudden you just end up following the flow, this internal perception of enjoyment that governs all your actions until you reach the top of the mountain.

A freedom manager will have to search for people who can mentor him/her by sharing their experiences on liberating themselves and their organizations from the constraints which we self-impose or are imposed by the organizations to which we belong. The other alternative is to look for individuals who have been less socialized into thinking organizations need to be as they are. It is common for organizations to take advantage of outsiders entering the workforce, usually younger colleagues, to promote fresh thinking and change. Some companies have formally established reverse mentoring programs where newly-hired employees mentor top managers on issues like new technologies, societal changes, and the like. In an analogous manner, freedom managers might take the opportunity to spend time with newly-hired colleagues and be exposed to the emerging values that Inglehart (2015) described as part of his description of post-materialism in new generations.

Becoming a freedom manager is a complex process of personal renovation where you will have to give up many assumptions on what your role needs to be. It is a challenge to be embraced with much courage, and the desire to make a real difference in the future of organizations. As such, it can be interpreted as a self-serving choice because of the belief that you need to act differently to keep enjoying the advantages of a prominent role. But it also entails a responsibility toward a different value system where individuals are set free from the constraints of organizations. Freedom managers will be the major actors of a paradigm shift in how we organize our society.

7.2 My company needs to change

Besides changing him/herself, a freedom manager will have to embrace the challenge of transforming organizations. While part of this challenge will be dealt with by the ongoing changes at the societal level, facilitated by the ubiquity of the new technologies which allow us to communicate, work, and decide in completely different ways, the complete transformation of organizations will still require individual actors taking the lead.

When confronted with the organizations that we inhabit today, it is difficult to believe that they can be transformed so radically in a few years. Command and control are still at the heart of the majority of organizations, and management roles tend to be rather traditional. However, it should be noted that many of the aforementioned changes have already been accomplished, albeit by only a few organizations or in a limited area of several organizations. The hype that surrounds start-ups and innovation is a relatively recent phenomenon, and an increasing share of the brightest and most inspired young generation is not willing to comply with the constraints of traditional organizations. They have already embraced the idea that they want to be the protagonists of their own futures. They are looking for new ways to combine their ideals, desires, and values with the need to produce enough economic resources to promote their well-being. And many of them are extraordinarily successful in doing so. In what organization could a 25-year-old person like Roman Kirsch (a German entrepreneur who at 22 sold Berlin-based online shopping club Casacanda to American design eCommerce site Fab for 10 million dollars) attain what he has achieved? And are you sure that if Mark Zuckerberg been one of your employees, he could have changed the world?

Interestingly, many of the founders of organizations which happen to change the world radically tend to be non-conformists who leave college before graduating in search of something more meaningful and more innovative and relevant. Do you really think they would find your company policies attractive or wait in line while you promote their senior colleagues because of their tenure?

a. Transform your HR

Organizations are made to follow rules, to define standards, to make sure people comply with them precisely because it is difficult to manage when one has to take responsibility for one's decisions on a daily basis. And the cornerstone of all this structure of constraints is usually the HR department, which despite all the hype on being a business partner is still acting as a loyal watchdog of customs and traditions.

Because how HR is organized deeply influences organizations, I suggest starting by refocusing this function. I equate the transformation that is needed to the difference between two approaches to the study of the natural world. On the one hand, geology is concerned with analysis of the stable structure of the Earth, and relies on the stratification in time to analyze how changes have occurred. On the other hand, ecology concentrates on the relationships between the environment and living things, and the pattern of interactions

Table 7.2 HR from geology to ecology

	Geology	Ecology
Role	– Loosely coupled roles – Business partner, shared services, center of expertise, etc. – *Support* management	– Integrated problem solving – Ad hoc teams & administrative support – *Inspire* management
Tools and practices	– Employee contract – Normative performance management – Talent framing and attribution – Training and development – Job description framing – Succession planning	– Tours of duty – Conversational performance management – Talent hunting – Development for self-guided learning and discovery – Job laboratory – Succession hiking
Competencies	– Standardization & control – Traditional business management – Formalization – Conformism	– Discovery & research – Experimentation – Multidisciplinary – Innovation and social innovation – Challenge
Ideology	Implicit behaviorism	Educated humanism
Epistemology	Normative	Collaborative management research

among different species in the same environment. In the same vein, traditional HR concentrates on a static view of people processes, while the HR of the future will have to be more concerned with the relational and dynamic nature of people processes (Table 7.2).

While in traditional HR the *role* is generally speaking to support management, thereby renouncing the idea of pursuing a specific agenda on human capital with a long-term people strategy, the new HR function will have to inspire management. Freedom managers will seek the competence and diagnostic ability of HR experts as important resources to support their activities. In this perspective, the HR function will have to focus on an integrated framework for people management decisions, instead of being loosely coupled and organized into separate units as in the shared service model so common today.

Consistently with a focus on exploration, *tools and practices* will have to be renovated. The notion of the employee contract with its emphasis on the long-term commitment of one or both parties will be substituted by the need to assign tours of duty which are meaningful and build upon the learning and experience of employees. In doing so, the HR function will have to work inside-out, being closely connected to the business and the employees to grasp the opportunities for new assignments and support employees in their journeys through different challenges. Consistently, performance management will need to give way to an ongoing conversation between individuals and their colleagues, where freedom managers, with the help of a renovated HR function, will be in charge of discovering valuable individuals to nurture and support, liberating them to accomplish more. Their role as managers will be to engage in talent hunting, which is a search for talents as they emerge from real experiences very different from the structured and rigid systems which are used today. Learning and development will take the form of quests initiated by individuals and supported by colleagues, peers, freedom managers, HR specialists, and external sources with a distinctive individual responsibility for self-learning. Job descriptions designed by experts will be replaced by shared platforms where people post descriptions of their activities and collaboratively redesign them on the basis of collectively defined needs or emerging opportunities. Design will morph into a social, collective, and collaborative activity. Finally, succession planning will lose the form of a structured approach to defining future leaders, which is seldom the basis for real promotion decisions, to embrace the idea of succession hiking sessions where valuable employees are exposed to conversations on their future plans and ideas for personal and organizational development.

The new HR function will require investment in novel *competencies* more consistent with the new organizational context. Central to them will be the same focus on discovery and search that I have described as a key competence of freedom managers. HR specialists will engage in research within the organization to discover talents and ideas for change. Experimentation with the tools and approaches to people development will require a multi-disciplinary background. Risk taking and desire for challenges, together with HR analytics, will sustain innovation.

Even more important is the shift needed in terms of approach and attitude in the *ideology* of HR. While HR managers tend to rely on an implicit behaviorism whereby they believe that they can influence individuals' behaviors by virtue of external incentives, the new HR manager will be an educated humanist recognizing the complexity of the motives that constitute a human being. Instead of believing in the ability to influence others, the HR managers and specialists will accept the fact that people are self-directed and need to be fully engaged in a course of action to embrace it. As a consequence, the HR function will need to change its *epistemology*, or the way in which learning about HR-related phenomena occurs. While most HR professionals tend to rely on normative assumptions on what works best, reinforced by consultants, the future of HR lies in the ability to engage in collaborative management research projects, where insiders are helped to define rigorous ways of learning from experience and research by outsiders characterized by a strong desire to support relevant actions.

b. Embrace risk taking and mistakes

As a consequence of the change in the way you define your people strategy, to embrace the metaphor of ecology a further change will involve disseminating a culture that reinforces learning from mistakes. Instead of thinking that organizations are error-proof systems, you need to cultivate errors as part of an ever-learning organization. Even more than accepting the idea of positive mistakes, your organization will have to urge people to take calculated risks in order to learn from them.

Although errors are not welcome in most organizations, it is only by building upon them that innovation can be promoted in order to help the organization free the energies of its members.

The fact that organizations in the future will be network-based and not reliant on hierarchy and control requires accepting the fact that some processes may at times be less effective. The trade-off between effectiveness and innovation will be resolved in time through the constant adjustment promoted by the self-reinforcing nature of collaborative processes, but it will occasionally start from solutions which may be highly ineffective or burdensome.

By designing an error-welcoming organization, individuals who have long felt pressure to conform will be allowed to see an open space for the expression of their ideas and values. Once again, the role of the HR function will be to support such an environment and to populate it with members who are heterogeneous and diverse and consequently able to promote real change continuously.

c. Remove evaluation, promote inspiration

The pressure to conform is one of the major enemies of the coming change in organizations. The ways in which we attract, hire, and evaluate members of the organization are embedded in assumptions on what is acceptable and what is considered not appropriate. However, all those tools activate a process whereby the ability of individuals to contribute differently is severely limited. While the change in the role and tools of the HR function will be instrumental to creating a different context, a central role in promoting standardization has always been played by performance management. The way in which organizations evaluate employees is a powerful exercise in conformism, and one imbued with rituality and power support.

This process can be easily equated with societal rituals. In fact, it is a process that binds all participants to the organization. It occurs on a recurrent basis, usually yearly, and prescribes a set of actions to be taken collectively. It is highly visible, and everybody in the organization is somehow affected and perceives the tension associated with it. It is segmented by levels, and requires that top managers gather together to define their collective judgments through mysterious calibration meetings. As a consequence of the process, some individuals are rewarded, others are even promoted to higher ranks, while the vast majority receive feedback on their value to the organization.

Dismantling this ritual is a necessity because it will send out the clear message that conformism is not the real target for organizational members. Evaluation assumes a much more relative meaning when people are not confronted with an ideal-typical definition of performance. Evaluation will have to give way to feedback which may come in many different forms but sees the individual as central. It is the individual that asks for the feedback to use it to reinforce him/herself and engage in actions to improve. This will be very different from the customary process governed by the HR function and administered by managers in a typical top-down manner.

d. Restructure the mindset of your managers

If you have followed this book all the way to this final chapter, you are probably convinced that a change is needed, and I can assume you will undertake the complex process of transformation into a freedom manager. The problem is that you are not likely to be alone in your organization, and as we have seen, the complexity of the change requires a sustained effort which is difficult if you are not supported.

The best scenario is one in which you are at the helm of the organization and have legitimate power to initiate change. In this case, your first act should be to design learning journeys that let your managers discover what lies ahead. Take them out of their comfort zones by exposing them to the idea that this book has generated in you. You have to challenge them to think that their future is at stake if they do not attempt to change. At the same time, you might consider defining a learning and development program to support the spread of the new competencies. Many of the actions that have applied to you can be extended to them in order to promote their changes.

A slightly more problematic scenario is one where you are a member of the organization while your top management has not yet embraced the idea of change. In this case, you can either try to sponsor the idea that radical change is needed or attempt to test some changes within your unit and/or office in the hope of being able to leverage them to convince the top management. Given the viral nature of liberty, any attempt at liberating the energy of individuals will easily spread through the organization and create interest. Whether or not your top management will embrace it will not depend only on the hype that you create; a positive pilot test will always be helpful.

7.3 Society needs to change

The coming change in organizations is more than a consequence of the competitive landscape and the evolution of the economy. As I have sought to show, it is the consequence of a long process of the individual's liberation from the physical and mental chains of tradition and social conformism. The constitution of societies has been a phenomenal accomplishment of humanity, but it has been accompanied by the need to limit individuals and their expression. Part of this has been a consequence of the need to enhance self-awareness among a broader stratum of humanity, which has led to the formalization of socialization processes (schools, colleges, military training, etc.), and part of it has been a side-effect of the creation of big, complex organizations according to the principle of hierarchy.

The further step in this process requires breaking free from the above-mentioned constraints. While reshaping your organization will be an important advance, you should consider the necessity of transforming this advance into a societal change. Apart from an ideological reason, it will be necessary because if the organizations of the future are to thrive, they will need to operate in a context where the same processes of liberation are in action.

It is for this reason that this concluding section indicates some actions to be undertaken outside the boundaries of your organization and extended to the society of which you are part.

a. Reshape education, it does not work

Traditional education systems are the strongholds of modern societies. They impose a dominant learning model which must be followed by everybody. While I recognize the superior value of education, and the fact that the existing education systems have been imposed to enable every citizen to acquire the means to act as a full citizen, the emphasis on a dominant learning model does not suffice to assure that knowledge is adequate to what we will face in the coming years.

Knowledge domains are continuously changing and their interactions are more complicated than ever, while our learning models are still based on the idea that we can separate liberal arts from science or mathematics from history. New scientific domains, like neurosciences, are characterized by convergence across different scientific fields.

Explore the link below for a map of science (Bollen et al., 2009). www.flickr.com/photos/dullhunk/3677405185

The organizations of the future will need competencies which span across many different domains, and a highly structured education system may not be ideally suited to developing them. An example of the challenges ahead is the difficult process by which organizations are trying to recruit and develop data scientists to help them take advantage of big data. While a key component of the role is the ability to use mathematical and statistical tools, the sheer complexity of the problems to be analyzed requires these roles to have a command of some aspects of how databases are created within IT systems. Moreover, data scientists need to understand the nature of the business problems that they have to address. Hence they cannot be only "crunching numbers" experts. The complexity of a role like this makes it evident that the specialization of education systems is not flexible to the hybridization of knowledge that society requires.

The emergence of alternative learning paradigms like the Singularity University or Minerva is a clear sign of the need for a profound revision of how learning is designed. From the focus on contents sharply separated by disciplinary boundaries, we need to invest in relations and links across disciplines and domains. Since no model can be defined, the best solution is once again to let spontaneous order emerge by making learners responsible for their learning and development.

b. Participatory democracy

The centrality of the individual is a great responsibility for each of us, but it also requires investment in the capacity to reach collective decisions whenever needed and when we cannot wait for spontaneous order to emerge and consolidate.

When organizations become collective minds connected through experiences and collaborative goals, how we decide on our everyday political and social lives will soon be perceived as outdated. The idea of the progressive centralization of power, which is at the roots of modern democracies due to the need to find effective ways to economize on collective decisions, can be discussed. The emergence of practices, tools and software designed to allow large numbers of people to examine problems collectively and reach a decision is giving rise to participatory social and political processes.

Participatory democracy is a form of collective problem-solving which avoids use of the shortcut of representation through elected bodies and brings issues back to individuals and communities. The existence of software which supports such processes, for example Synthetron or LiquidFeedback, dramatically increases the ability to collect ideas and involve large numbers of individuals. Apart from promoting the same processes within your organization, the diffusion of them in society will allow people to acquire the capacity to sustain collaborative processes. Moreover, if you believe as I do that structured involvement leads to better decisions, corporate leaders should use their influence to promote such changes, instead of partnering or lobbying with political parties interested in maintaining their representation power in society.

c. Reduce barriers to change, and create experimentation areas in your country

In most countries, corporate leaders are part of the elite, so you probably share responsibility for decisions affecting your nation. Most of the systems blocking change can be reduced by opening up alternatives or promoting experimentation. The advent of a freer society requires an effort to overcome numerous barriers. First, you should consider the amount of talent that goes unexploited simply because young, bright individuals are not given the chance fully to express their potential. You and your company might be important actors in searching for these hidden gems and promoting their education in a manner very similar to what has happened to the actors of the world-renowned Indian movie *Slumdog Millionaire*, featuring the story of a young Indian boy participating in the TV show *Who Wants to Be a Millionaire?*.

Another contribution will be to create opportunities for experimentation and research to flourish outside the constraints of traditional research institutions, which tend to be rather conformist in their approach to innovation. The diffusion of hackathon events is an example of how you could organize these settings. Fostering the spontaneous gathering of people with different ideas and competencies is a powerful tool with which to promote and ignite innovation and change.

While traditional venture capitalists invest money in ideas, your role could be that of a promoter investing in the infrastructure that sustains the emergence of start-ups and new initiatives.

7.4 Final thoughts

I have followed my path as an academic, being part of the rites of this community. However, I have always felt the need to reflect on the relationship between the rigor of how academic research needs to be developed and the problem of relevance, and impact.

As time went by I grew progressively less satisfied with what I perceived as limits to academics. The constant struggle to legitimize our research and be acknowledged induces us to pursue research for the sake of publishing in increasingly prestigious journals.

There is nothing wrong with this, believe me. It requires strong discipline; you need to be very bright, probably among the brightest, and some research products are masterpieces in the real sense of the word.

The problem for me was that as I was struggling to become an academic, I perceived that the role model was different from the role model of other social scientists, like Max Weber, that I had in my personal academic Valhalla. While they were deeply embedded in the debate of their times, we tend to be constrained within an ivory tower to which only the pure are admitted. While I rejected the idea of a militant social scientist, being very much in tune with Weber, I thought that research had to concentrate on what was happening in the larger society, and maybe attempt to anticipate changes instead of following them, creating intriguing models of what has happened but with no explanations as to why it has happened and how it could evolve in the future.

For this reason, I collected notes from keynote speeches on the future of management and the many spontaneous conversations with friends and occasional encounters at companies' events and training programs. From time to time, I would go through some of them and maybe write a blog entry on The Corporate SenseMaker blog (http://lucasolari.com/) or take advantage of LinkedIn Pulse. The idea of converting those random thoughts and ideas into a book was far from my mind. As a traditional academic, I thought that combining rigor with innovation would lead me on a very narrow path between two dangerous slopes: on the one side the slope of irrelevance, where I would talk to fellow academics but lose myself in far-fetched ideas rather obscure to practitioners; on the other side, the much feared slope of non-rigorous theorizing which would have me perceived as a weird kind of academic. Approaching the end of this book, I am not sure that I have kept the right balance, and I hope I have not fallen down both slopes at once.

However, as I have tried to express in the pages of this book, I believe in taking risks and fighting to let your ideas and values emerge. This book is my way of breaking free from the chains of habit. It recommends its readers to look further into the future, revising their perceptions of the present.

But the next page is not mine to write: it will appear in the actions that will change our organizations, our society, and hopefully our way of co-existing on this planet.

Bibliography

Alvesson, M., and Willmott, H., 1995. Strategic management as domination and emancipation: From planning and process to communication and praxis. *Advances in Strategic Management* 12, 85–112.

An executive's guide to machine learning | McKinsey & Company [WWW Document], 2015. URL: www.mckinsey.com/insights/high_tech_telecoms_internet/an_executives_guide_to_machine_learning (accessed 8.25.15).

Artificial intelligence meets the C-suite | McKinsey & Company [WWW Document], 2014. URL: www.mckinsey.com/business-functions/strategy-and-corporate-finance/our-insights/artificial-intelligence-meets-the-c-suite (accessed 8.25.15).

Augier, M., 1999. Some notes on Alfred Schütz and the Austrian School of Economics: Review of Alfred Schütz's Collected Papers, Vol. IV. Edited by H. Wagner, G. Psathas and F. Kersten (1996). *The Review of Austrian Economics* 11, 145–162.

Bainbridge, W.S., 2007. The scientific research potential of virtual worlds. *Science* 317, 472–476.

Baker, W. 1992. The network organization in theory and practice. In Nohria, N. and Eccles, R. G. (eds), *Networks and Organizations*. Boston, MA: Harvard Business School Press.

Barnard, C.I., 1938. *The Functions of the Executive*. Cambridge MA: Harvard University Press.

Barney, J., 1991. Firm resources and sustained competitive advantage. *Journal of Management* 17, 99–120. doi:10.1177/014920639101700108

Bartlett, C.A., and Ghoshal, S., 1993. Beyond the M-form: Toward a managerial theory of the firm. *Strategic Management Journal* 14, 23–46.

Bauman, Z., 2000. *Liquid Modernity*, 1st ed. Cambridge: Polity.

Beck, U., 1992. *Risk Society: Towards a New Modernity*, 1st ed. London: SAGE Publications Ltd.

Berg, J.M., Dutton, J.E., and Wrzesniewski, A., 2008. What is job crafting and why does it matter? Retrieved from the website of Positive Organizational Scholarship on April 15, 2011 (http://positiveorgs.bus.umich.edu/wp-content/uploads/What-is-Job-Crafting-and-Why-Does-it-Matter1.pdf).

Berger, P.L., and Luckmann, T., 1967. *The Social Construction of Reality: A Treatise in the Sociology of Knowledge*. New York: Anchor.

Blake, R.R., and Mouton, J.S., 1964. *The Managerial Grid*. Houston: Gulf Publishing.

Bollen, J., Van de Sompel, H., Hagberg, A., Bettencourt, L., Chute, R., Rodriguez, M.A., and Balakireva, L., 2009. Clickstream Data Yields High-Resolution Maps of Science. *PLoS ONE* 4, e4803. doi:10.1371/journal.pone.0004803.

Boulos, M.N.K., Hetherington, L., and Wheeler, S., 2007. Second Life: an overview of the potential of 3-D virtual worlds in medical and health education. *Health Information & Libraries Journal* 24, 233–245.

Brandenburger, A.M., and Nalebuff, B.J., 2011. *Co-opetition*. New York: Crown Business.

Braverman, H., 1998. *Labor and Monopoly Capital: The Degradation of Work in the Twentieth Century*, Anv. ed. New York: Monthly Review Press.

Broeck, A., Vansteenkiste, M., Witte, H., Soenens, B., and Lens, W., 2010. Capturing autonomy, competence, and relatedness at work: Construction and initial validation of the Work-related Basic Need Satisfaction scale. *Journal of Occupational and Organizational Psychology* 83, 981–1002.

Burawoy, M., 1982. *Manufacturing Consent: Changes in the Labor Process under Monopoly Capitalism*, Paperback Edition 1982. ed. University of Chicago Press.

Burns, T.E., and Stalker, G.M., 1961. The management of innovation. University of Illinois at Urbana-Champaign's Academy for Entrepreneurial Leadership Historical Research Reference in Entrepreneurship.

Cappelli, P., 2008. Talent management for the twenty-first century. *Harvard Business Review* 86, 74.

Carroll, G.R., and Hannan, M.T., 2000. *The Demography of Corporations and Industries*. Princeton University Press.

Carter, M., and Gibbs, M.R., 2013. eSports in EVE Online: Skullduggery, fair play and acceptability in an unbounded competition. In *Proceedings of the Foundations of Digital Games 2013*, Society for the Advancement of the Science of Digital Games, pp. 47–54.

Castells, M., 1996. *Rise of the Network Society* (Information Age Series), 1st ed. Oxford: Wiley-Blackwell.

Chandler, A.D., 1977. *The Visible Hand: The Managerial Revolution in American Business*. Cambridge MA: Harvard University Press.

Davies, J., 2014. Philips digital innovation chief Alberto Prado outlines 4 core steps for businesses undergoing digital transformation [WWW Document]. *The Drum*. URL: www.thedrum.com/news/2014/11/21/philips-digital-innovation-chief-alberto-prado-outlines-4-core-steps-businesses (accessed 7.31.15).

DiIorio, F., 2013. Hayek's The Sensory Order and Gadamer's Phenomenological Hermeneutics. CHOPE Center for the History of Political Economy at Duke University Working Paper.

Drucker, P.F., 1989. What business can learn from nonprofits. *Harvard Business Review* 67(4), 88–93.

Estrin, J., 2015. Kodak's First Digital Moment [WWW Document]. Lens Blog, *New York Times*. URL: http://lens.blogs.nytimes.com/2015/08/12/kodaks-first-digital-moment/ (accessed 8.20.15).

Fayol, H., and Gray, I., 1984. *General and Industrial Management*, Rev Sub. ed. New York: IEEE.

Feng, W., Brandt, D., and Saha, D., 2007. A long-term study of a popular MMORPG, in: *Proceedings of the 6th ACM SIGCOMM Workshop on Network and System Support for Games*. ACM, pp. 19–24.

Fiedler, F.E., 1967. *A Theory of Leadership Effectiveness*. New York: McGraw-Hill.

Foucault, M., 1995. *Discipline & Punish: The Birth of the Prison*, 2nd ed. New York; Vintage.

Galbraith, J.R., 1995. *Designing Organizations: An Executive Briefing on Strategy, Structure, and Process.* San Francisco: Jossey-Bass.

Gehlen, A., 1989. *Man in the Age of Technology.* New York: Columbia University Press.

Gelles, D., 2015. At Zappos, Pushing Shoes and a Vision. *The New York Times.* Available at www.nytimes.com/2015/07/19/business/at-zappos-selling-shoes-and-a-vision.html?_r=0.

Ghoshal, S., 2005. Bad management theories are destroying good management practices. *Academy of Management Learning & Education* 4, 75–91.

Giddens, A., 1986. *The Constitution of Society: Outline of the Theory of Structuration.* University of California Press.

Gratton, L., 2011. *The Shift: The Future of Work Is Already Here.* London: HarperCollins UK.

Grove, A.S., 1999. *Only the Paranoid Survive: How to Exploit the Crisis Points That Challenge Every Company,* Reprint edition. ed. New York: Crown Business.

Guetzkow, H., and Simon, H.A., 1955. The impact of certain communication nets upon organization and performance in task-oriented groups. *Management Science* 1, 233–250.

Hackman, J.R., and Oldham, G.R., 1976. Motivation through the design of work: Test of a theory. *Organizational Behavior and Human Performance* 16, 250–279.

Hayek, F.A., 1978. *The Constitution of Liberty.* Chicago: The University of Chicago Press.

Hayek, F.A.V., 2005. *The Road to Serfdom: With the Intellectuals and Socialism.* London: Institute of Economic Affairs.

Hey, T., 2010. The next scientific revolution. *Harvard Business Review* 88, 56–63.

Hoffman, R., Casnocha, B., and Yeh, C., 2014. *The Alliance: Managing Talent in the Networked Age.* Boston: Harvard Business Review Press.

Husserl, E., 1970. The Crisis of European Sciences and Transcendental Phenomenology: An Introduction to Phenomenological Philosophy. Evanston: Northwestern University Press.

Inglehart, R., 2015. *The Silent Revolution: Changing Values and Political Styles Among Western Publics.* Princeton University Press.

Inglehart, R., and Welzel, C., 2010. Changing mass priorities: The link between modernization and democracy. *Perspectives on Politics* 8, 551–567.

Kapell, M.W., 2010. *Star Trek as Myth: Essays on Symbol and Archetype at the Final Frontier.* London: McFarland.

Keidel, R.W., 1995. *Seeing Organizational Patterns: A New Theory and Language of Organizational Design.* San Francisco: Berrett-Koehler Publishers.

Kemp, J., and Livingstone, D., 2006. Putting a Second Life "metaverse" skin on learning management systems, in: *Proceedings of the Second Life Education Workshop at the Second Life Community Convention.* San Francisco: The University of Paisley CA.

Kim, W.C., and Mauborgne, R., 2005. *Blue Ocean Strategy: How to Create Uncontested Market Space and Make the Competition Irrelevant.* Boston: Harvard Business School Press.

Kniberg, H., and Ivarsson, A., 2012. Scaling Agile @ Spotify. Available at https://ucvox.files.wordpress.com/2012/11/113617905-scaling-agile-spotify-11.pdf.

Lawrence, P.R., and Lorsch, J.W., 1967. Differentiation and integration in complex organizations. *Administrative Science Quarterly* 12(1), 1–47.

Leonardi, P.M., 2011. When flexible routines meet flexible technologies: Affordance, constraint, and the imbrication of human and material agencies. *MIS Quarterly* 35, 147–167.

Leonardi, P.M., Huysman, M., and Steinfield, C., 2013. Enterprise social media: Definition, history, and prospects for the study of social technologies in organizations. *Journal of Computer-Mediated Communication* 19, 1–19.

Mackenzie, K.D., 1991. The organizational hologram, in: *The Organizational Hologram: The Effective Management of Organizational Change*. Netherlands: Springer, pp. 3–23.

Mansfield, R.S., 1996. Building competency models: Approaches for HR professionals. *Human Resource Management* 35, 7.

Manzolini, L., Soda, G., and Solari, L., 1994. *L'organizzazione snella*. Milano: Etas.

March, J.G., 1991. Exploration and exploitation in organizational learning. *Organization Science* 2, 71–87.

Marx, K., 1967. *Capital: A Critical Analysis of Capitalist Production: The Process of Capitalist Production*. New York: International Publishers Co.

Mason, M.F., Cloutier, J., and Macrae, C.N., 2006. On construing others: Category and stereotype activation from facial cues. *Social Cognition* 24, 540–562.

Mayo, E., 1949. Hawthorne and the western electric company. From Elton Mayo, *The Social Problems of an Industrial Civilization*. Boston: Division of Research, Harvard Business School.

McGonigal, J., and Whelan, J., 2012. *Reality is Broken: Why Games Make Us Better and How They Can Change the World*, Unabridged ed. London: Brilliance Audio.

McPherson, J.M., and Smith-Lovin, L., 1987. Homophily in voluntary organizations: Status distance and the composition of face-to-face groups. *American Sociological Review* 52, 370–379.

McPherson, M., Smith-Lovin, L., and Cook, J.M., 2001. Birds of a feather: Homophily in social networks. *Annual Review of Sociology* 27, 415–444.

Moorehead, C., 1994. The odyssey of Heinrich Schliemann: The uncovering of the city of Troy was one of archaeology's great moments; the discovery of its golden treasure one of the great rewards. Schliemann found it. His wife Sophia wore it. For the first time in 50 years the world is about to see it. Caroline Moorehead tells his story [WWW Document]. *The Independent*. URL: www.independent. co.uk/life-style/the-odyssey-of-heinrich-schliemann-the-uncovering-of-the-city-of-troy-was-one-of-archaeologys-great-moments-the-discovery-of-its-golden-treasure-one-of-the-great-rewards-schliemann-found-it-his-wife-sophia-wore-it-for-the-first-time-in-50-years-the-world-is-about-to-see-it-caroline-moorehead-tells-his-story-1445558.html (accessed 8.27.15).

NPR, 2015. Zappos: A workplace where no one and everyone is the boss. URL: www.npr.org/2015/07/21/421148128/zappos-a-workplace-where-no-one-and-everyone-is-the-boss (accessed 4.13.16).

Orlikowski, W.J., 2009. The sociomateriality of organisational life: considering technology in management research. Cambridge Journal of Economics 34, 125–141.

Orpen, C., 1994. The effects of organizational and individual career management on career success. International Journal of Manpower 15, 27–37.

Ouchi, W.G., 1984. The m-form society: Lessons from business management. Human Resource Management 23, 191–213.

Paul, C.A., 2011. Don't play me: EVE Online, new players and rhetoric, in: Proceedings of the 6th International Conference on Foundations of Digital Games. ACM, pp. 262–264.

Peters, T.J., 1992. Liberation Management: Necessary Disorganization for the Nanosecond Nineties. New York: Random House.

Petsoulas, C., 2013. Hayek's Liberalism and Its Origins: His Idea of Spontaneous Order and the Scottish Enlightenment, Reprint ed. London: Routledge.

Porter, M.E., 2008. Competitive Advantage: Creating and Sustaining Superior Performance. New York: Simon and Schuster.

Prahalad, C.K., and Hamel, G., 1990. The core competence of the corporation. Harvard Business Review 68, 79–91.

Rao, H., Morrill, C., and Zald, M.N., 2000. Power plays: How social movements and collective action create new organizational forms. Research in Organizational Behavior 22, 237–281.

Rheingold, H., 1992. Virtual Reality: The Revolutionary Technology of Computer-Generated Artificial Worlds – and How It Promises to Transform Society. New York: Simon & Schuster.

Roberts, J., 2007. The Modern Firm: Organizational Design for Performance and Growth. Oxford: Oxford University Press.

Rothbard, M.N., 1976. Praxeology: The methodology of Austrian economics. In Dolan, E.G. (ed.) The Foundations of Modern Austrian Economics. Kansas City: Sheed and Ward, pp. 19–39.

Ryan, R.M., and Deci, E.L., 2000. Self-determination theory and the facilitation of intrinsic motivation, social development, and well-being. American Psychologist 55, 68–78. doi:10.1037/0003-066X.55.1.68

Rymaszewski, M., 2007. Second Life: The Official Guide. Hoboken: John Wiley & Sons.

Schumpeter, J.A., 2013. Capitalism, Socialism and Democracy. Abingdon: Routledge.

Schutz, A., 1970. Alfred Schutz on Phenomenology and Social Relations. University of Chicago Press.

Selgin, G.A., 1988. Praxeology and understanding: An analysis of the controversy in Austrian economics. The Review of Austrian Economics 2, 19–58.

Seligman, M.E., and Csikszentmihalyi, M., 2000. Positive psychology: An introduction. American Psychologist 55(1), 5–14.

Sennett, R., 2000. The Corrosion of Character: The Personal Consequences of Work in the New Capitalism, 1st ed. New York: W. W. Norton & Company.

Shani, A.B.R., Mohrman, S.A., Pasmore, W.A., Stymne, B., and Adler, N., 2007. Handbook of Collaborative Management Research. Los Angeles: SAGE Publications.

Sheldon, K.M., Elliot, A.J., Ryan, R.M., Chirkov, V., Kim, Y., Wu, C., Demir, M., and Sun, Z., 2004. Self-concordance and subjective well-being in four cultures. Journal of Cross-Cultural Psychology 35, 209–223.

Sheldon, K.M., and Ryan, R.M., 2011. Positive psychology and self-determination theory: A natural interface. In Chirkov, V.I., Ryan, R.M., and Sheldon, K.M. (eds), Human Autonomy in Cross-Cultural Context, Cross-Cultural Advancements in Positive Psychology. Dordrecht: Springer, pp. 33–44.

Shen, C., 2013. Network patterns and social architecture in Massively Multiplayer Online Games: Mapping the social world of EverQuest II. New Media & Society doi: 10.1177/1461444813489507.

Simmel, G., 1972. Georg Simmel on Individuality and Social Forms. University Of Chicago Press.

Solari, L., 2014. The relationship between management and capitalism from a critical history of modernity point of view: Janus, the two faced God vs. Yin-Yang. In Kazeroony, H. and Stachowicz-Stanusch, A. (eds) Capitalism and the

Social Relationship: An Organizational Perspective. Basingstoke: Palgrave Macmillan.

Spreitzer, G.M., 1995. Psychological empowerment in the workplace: Dimensions, measurement, and validation. Academy of Management Journal 38, 1442–1465.

Stinchcombe, A.L., 1965. Social structure and organizations In March, J.G. (ed.) Handbook of Organizations. Chicago: Rand McNally, pp. 142–193.

Sugden, R., 1989. Spontaneous order. The Journal of Economic Perspectives 3(4), 85–97.

Szell, M., Lambiotte, R., and Thurner, S., 2010. Multirelational organization of large-scale social networks in an online world. Proceedings of the National Academy of Sciences 107, 13636–13641.

Taylor, F.W., 2006. The Principles of Scientific Management. New York: Cosimo Classics.

Taylor, F.W., 1947. Scientific Management: Comprising Shop management, The principles of scientific management and Testimony before the special House committee. New York: Harper.

Thaler, R.H., and Sunstein, C.R., 2009. Nudge: Improving Decisions About Health, Wealth, and Happiness, Revised & Expanded ed. New York: Penguin Books.

Thompson, J.D., 2011. Organizations in Action: Social Science Bases of Administrative Theory. New Brunswick: Transaction Publishers.

Turner, J.H., 1997. The Institutional Order: Economy, Kinship, Religion, Polity, Law, and Education in Evolutionary and Comparative Perspective. New York: Longman.

van Wyhe, J., Carroll, A., 2011. Charles Darwin: A life of discovery. In Hutchins M. (ed.), Grzimek's Animal Life Evolution. Farmington Hills, MI: Gale, pp. 31–44.

Warburton, S., 2009. Second Life in higher education: Assessing the potential for and the barriers to deploying virtual worlds in learning and teaching. British Journal of Educational Technology 40, 414–426.

Weber, M., 2010. The Protestant Ethic and the Spirit of Capitalism. CreateSpace Independent Publishing Platform.

Weick, K.E., 1995. Sensemaking in Organizations. Thousand Oaks: SAGE.

Williamson, O.E., 1989. Transaction cost economics. In Schmalensee, R. and Willig, R. (eds) Handbook of Industrial Organization, vol. 1. Oxford: Elsevier, pp. 135–182.

Index

Page numbers in **bold** indicate figures and tables.

Taylor & Francis eBooks

Helping you to choose the right eBooks for your Library

Add Routledge titles to your library's digital collection today. Taylor and Francis ebooks contains over 50,000 titles in the Humanities, Social Sciences, Behavioural Sciences, Built Environment and Law.

Choose from a range of subject packages or create your own!

Benefits for you

» Free MARC records
» COUNTER-compliant usage statistics
» Flexible purchase and pricing options
» All titles DRM-free.

REQUEST YOUR FREE INSTITUTIONAL TRIAL TODAY

Free Trials Available
We offer free trials to qualifying academic, corporate and government customers.

Benefits for your user

» Off-site, anytime access via Athens or referring URL
» Print or copy pages or chapters
» Full content search
» Bookmark, highlight and annotate text
» Access to thousands of pages of quality research at the click of a button.

eCollections – Choose from over 30 subject eCollections, including:

Archaeology	Language Learning
Architecture	Law
Asian Studies	Literature
Business & Management	Media & Communication
Classical Studies	Middle East Studies
Construction	Music
Creative & Media Arts	Philosophy
Criminology & Criminal Justice	Planning
Economics	Politics
Education	Psychology & Mental Health
Energy	Religion
Engineering	Security
English Language & Linguistics	Social Work
Environment & Sustainability	Sociology
Geography	Sport
Health Studies	Theatre & Performance
History	Tourism, Hospitality & Events

For more information, pricing enquiries or to order a free trial, please contact your local sales team:
www.tandfebooks.com/page/sales

 Routledge
Taylor & Francis Group

The home of
Routledge books

www.tandfebooks.com